Leading YOU™

Also by Brenda Bence

Would YOU Want to Work for YOU™?
How to Build an Executive Leadership Brand that
Inspires Loyalty and Drives Employee Performance

Master the Brand Called YOU™
The Proven Leadership Personal Branding System to
Help You Earn More, Do More, and Be More at Work

Smarter Branding Without Breaking The Bank
Five Proven Marketing Strategies You Can Use Right Now to
Build Your Business at Little or No Cost

How YOU™ Are Like Shampoo for Job Seekers
The Proven Personal Branding System to Help You Succeed
in Any Interview and Secure the Job of Your Dreams

How YOU™ Are Like Shampoo for College Graduates
The Complete Personal Branding System to Define, Position,
and Market Yourself and Land a Job You Love

Branding Matters
How to Achieve Greater Success Through Powerhouse Branding
… For You, Your Products, and Your Company

Praise from around the world for *Leading YOU*™

"You may excel at managing others, but unless you look inward to manage yourself first, your career is likely to stagnate rather than ignite. *Leading YOU*™ is a must read."
 — Peter Walker, CEO Asia Pacific, ThyssenKrupp Elevator

"I recommend *Leading YOU*™ to anyone who is a leader—or aspires to be. As I look at myself and others in my profession, I can see that author Brenda Bence is right: Self-leadership *is the* missing piece for most of us. Brenda has been invaluable to me at critical points in my career, helping me bridge my current role with my aspirations. A decade later, I continue to view my work with Brenda as a true breakthrough moment."
 — Andrew Padovano, Managing Director, New York, Citi

"As executives, we are often taught skills for leading others, but Brenda Bence makes it clear that it's even more important to take charge of leading *ourselves*. *Leading YOU*™ underscores how critical self-leadership is to continuing success. This book will inspire you to take action and make positive change."
 — Angela Ryan, Chief HR & Talent Officer, APAC, GroupM

"What an enlightening book! It's practical and allows you to reflect on your self-leadership behaviors. In *Leading YOU*™, you'll find many tips that can be applied immediately in your professional *and* personal life. Pragmatic and useful."
 — Steven B. Binder, Vice President & CFO, Stryker International

"As a leader, it's easy to become so focused on team leadership that I don't put as much effort on *self*-leadership. But in *Leading YOU*™, Executive Coach Brenda Bence makes it clear that how I lead myself must come first. Extremely invaluable insights shared—definitely worth reading."
 — Melissa Ries, Vice President & General Manager, APAC, Skillsoft

"Almost every leader focuses on leading others. Brenda shows that self-leadership is just as important—maybe even more important—because it's the foundation of all leadership. This book is to the point, with a valuable and effective checklist to 'grow better,' thus motivating yourself and all others who surround YOU!"
 — Dale A. Martin, Chief Executive Officer, Siemens Hungary

"*Leading YOU*™ is unique. Filled with actual examples of self-leadership successes and failures, it's both a mirror and a map. Highly recommended!"
 — Leona Tan, Managing Director
   Community Affairs and Diversity & Inclusion, UBS AG, APAC

"After reading *Leading YOU™*, I realize that self-leadership is one of the most neglected areas of executive development. It is truly the key to becoming a better leader, as well as improving your overall quality of life—both at work and at home. The topics discussed here are not just theory but things that Brenda Bence puts into practice with top leaders in the industry."

— Ajit Varghese, CEO Asia Pacific, Maxus

"Executive Coach Brenda Bence has been in a position to see corporate leaders perform at their best … and at their worst. That unique bird's-eye view of the senior executive world allows her to share what helps those at the upper echelons of an organization get out of their own way. I will recommend this book to leaders—and aspiring leaders—at all levels!"

— Linda Eunson
  Director, Alumni/Corporate Relations and Career Management, Asia
  The University of Chicago Booth School of Business

"Brenda's books are so pragmatic and down-to-earth—you can immediately apply what she shares. And, they are also a wonderful reflection of her one-to-one approach to executive coaching. *Leading YOU™* is well worth reading!"

— Christoph Kurth, General Counsel Wealth Management APAC, UBS AG

"What I love about Brenda's books is that they're so practical and hands-on—she doesn't burden you with a lot of theory that's nice to read but hard to use. In *Leading YOU™*, you'll find dozens of tips that can be applied immediately in your day-to-day work world. Very useful and pragmatic."

— Jeff Ames, Managing Director, Asia Pacific, WEX Inc.

"Thanks to Brenda's latest book, I'm looking at leadership in a new light—*self*-leadership, that is. *Leading YOU™* will help you become a better example for others. I particularly appreciate the techniques shared around self-promotion without boasting and the powerful tips on mind management. When we change how we think as leaders, we can change most anything else. Thoroughly enjoyable read!"

— Patrecia Valone, Region Head
  Clinical Development Operations Singapore/Shanghai,
  Takeda Development Center Asia

"What a wise and practical book! I realize now how overlooking self-leadership behaviors can be a serious hindrance to anyone's career. In this book, Brenda walks you step by step through how to avoid potential self-leadership pitfalls. This book holds exciting prospects for leaders!"

— Angelia Kay, Regional Director, Asia Pacific, Garlock Sealing Technologies

Leading YOU™

The power of
SELF-LEADERSHIP
to build your executive brand
and drive career success

Brenda Bence
SENIOR EXECUTIVE COACH AND INTERNATIONAL BRANDING EXPERT

Copyright © 2017 by Brenda S. Bence. All rights reserved.

Published by Global Insight Communications LLC, Las Vegas, Nevada, U.S.A.

ISBN: 978-1-942718-01-7
Library of Congress Control Number: 2016952848

Cover design by George Foster, Foster Covers (www.fostercovers.com)
Interior design and typesetting by Eric Myhr
Graphics by Swas "Kwan" Siripong, Brenda Brown
Photos by Danielle Johnston (daniellejohnston.photo@gmail.com), Bergen Johnston (www.bergenjohnstonphotography.com) and Phil Nealey (www.nealeyphoto.com)

The stories in this book are based on real events and real people. To protect the privacy of individuals and companies, names and identifying details have been changed.

No part of this publication may be reproduced, stored in a retrieval system, or transmitted in any form or by any means, electronic, mechanical, photocopying, recording, scanning, or otherwise, without the prior written permission of the publisher. Requests to the publisher for permission should be addressed to the Permission Department, Global Insight Communications, P.O. Box 80267, Las Vegas, NV 89180, U.S.A. Phone: +1-312-242-1830 or by e-mail at info@globalinsightcommunications.com.

YOUTM (YOU™, YOU™, YOU™® or similar graphic illustration) is a registered trademark and service mark of Global Insight Communications, LLC and is protected by US and international trademark laws.

Limit of Liability/Disclaimer of Warranty: While the publisher and author have used their best efforts in preparing this book, they make no representations or warranties with respect to the accuracy or completeness of the contents of this book and specifically disclaim any implied warranties of merchantability or fitness for a particular purpose. No warranty may be created or extended by sales representatives or written sales materials. The advice and strategies contained herein may not be suitable for your situation. Neither the publisher nor author shall be liable for any loss of profit or any other commercial damages, including but not limited to special, incidental, consequential, or other damages.

Unless otherwise noted, all footnoted webpage references were last accessed in August 2016.

Publisher's Cataloging-in-Publication data:

Names: Bence, Brenda, author.
Title: Leading YOU : the power of self-leadership to build your executive brand and drive career success / Brenda Bence.
Description: Includes index. | Las Vegas, NV: Global Insight Communications, LLC: 2017
Identifiers: ISBN 978-1-942718-01-7 | LCCN 2016952848
Subjects: LCSH Leadership. | Success in business. | Executive ability. | Executives. | Career development. | BISAC BUSINESS & ECONOMICS / Leadership | BUSINESS & ECONOMICS / Marketing / General
Classification: LCC HD69.B7 B38 2017 | DDC 658.8/27--dc23

This book is dedicated to every executive coaching client I've had the privilege to work with throughout the years. I'm honored by the trust you have placed in me.

Contents

1. Leading Others Is Only Half the Story 11

   Top 15 Limiting Self-Leadership Behaviors:

   2. Believing You're a Victim at Work 27
   3. Not Managing Your Mind 37
   4. Getting Stuck in Black-and-White Thinking 45
   5. Devoting Little or No Time to Strategic Thinking 53
   6. Ignoring the Importance of Time Management 61
   7. Saying "Yes" When You Want to Say "No" 76
   8. Failing to Address Conflict When It Arises 86
   9. Not Being Ready for the Challenges of Today's Diverse Workplace .. 99
   10. Managing Down More Than Up and Across 115
   11. Overlooking the Importance of Executive Presence 128
   12. Underestimating the Significance of Self-Promotion and Visibility... 137
   13. Struggling with Tough Decisions 149
   14. Not Being Clear About Your Long-Term Career Aspirations 156
   15. Not Knowing How to Influence Without Authority 163
   16. Failing to Seek Regular and "Real" Feedback 175

17. Setting Self-Leadership Goals 182
18. Leading YOU™ to Success 190

    Index 201
    About the Author 209
    Acknowledgments 211
    Services Provided by Brenda Bence 213

1

Leading Others Is Only Half the Story

"Everyone thinks of changing the world, but no one thinks of changing himself."

— Leo Tolstoy, Russian Novelist

In *Would YOU Want to Work For YOU™?*, the companion book to *Leading YOU™*, I shared the top 15 *people*-leadership behaviors that I frequently see which prevent executives from becoming the kind of leader others want to follow. So, why would I write another book with 15 *more* behaviors that leaders need to work on?

For a very important reason: People-leadership behaviors are only one portion of an executive's journey. Yes, they are absolutely critical to success … but on their own, they are not enough to help you reach your full potential. Before you can effectively lead subordinates, you must first effectively *lead yourself*.

Self-leadership is the missing piece for so many executives— a key area of leadership that often gets neglected.

It's a little like the old saying, "You can't love someone else until you love yourself." Well, I'm convinced that you cannot successfully manage others until you're adept at managing your *own* mindset, actions, and reactions. Countless times, I've watched a lack of self-leadership derail the careers of otherwise promising executives. In contrast, when focus is placed on strengthening self-leadership, I've personally seen it turn around careers, save executives from losing their positions, shift leaders from being despised to being admired, and change entire corporate cultures.

That's why in *Leading YOU™*, I'll highlight the top 15 *self-leadership* behaviors that may be holding you back and preventing you from reaching your ultimate success as a leader. These are not always obvious or even conscious behaviors, but in my years serving as an Executive Coach to hundreds of senior executives around the globe, I've consistently seen these 15 as the most common self-leadership mistakes.

Life-Changing Advice That Taught Me the Importance of Self-Leadership

The importance of self-leadership became clear to me years ago, during an unexpected encounter with John Pepper, then-Chairman and CEO of Procter & Gamble (P&G). It was a hot August night in Cincinnati, Ohio, the home of P&G's world headquarters. I had just flown in the day before from China, where I was living and working for P&G as an expat, to attend a global meeting for the company's marketing leaders. Once the all-day event was over, I holed myself up in a corner of the darkened 9th floor—my old stomping grounds when I worked there—in order to catch up on emails.

Glancing at my watch, I realized it was almost 9:30 p.m., so I packed up my things to head back to the hotel. Making my way through a half-lit hallway, I reached the elevator bank and pushed the "down" button. As I glanced up, I realized the elevator was descending from the 11th floor.

Back then, the 11th floor of P&G's world headquarters was called "Mahogany Row" due to the beautiful mahogany desks that graced the space. Those desks belonged to the highest-level leaders in the multibillion-dollar corporation—P&G's C-Suite Executives: the CEO, the COO, the CFO, the CMO, the CIO, the C-I-E-I-O (you get my drift).

Standing there watching the elevator numbers counting down from 11 … to 10 … to 9, a thought flashed through my mind: "I wonder if anybody from the 11th floor will be sharing the car with me."

As if on cue, the elevator doors opened and, sure enough, there stood John Pepper. As I stepped inside, it suddenly hit me: I was going to have nine floors—count 'em, *nine*—of one-on-one time with the company's #1 executive.

Because I had presented to John many times, I knew he was aware that I was managing key company brands in Greater China, an important strategic location for the company. I also knew that, after 30 hours of long-haul travel and attending an all-day meeting, the pistons of my brain-engine weren't exactly hitting on all cylinders. That's when I heard inside my head the wise voice of one of my favorite mentors, saying, "Brenda, always be prepared with a question for upper management in case you run into them. Because if you don't ask *them* a question, they will ask *you* one."

So, to avoid being faced with a brain-challenging inquiry in my exhausted state, I turned and said, "Good evening, John. It's nice to see you. Do you mind if I ask you a question?"

"Not at all," he answered. "Feel free."

"There's something I've been wondering about," I said. "I understand what it takes to progress from Assistant Brand Manager to Brand Manager. And I'm clear about what's required to move from Brand Manager to Associate Marketing Manager and from there to Marketing Manager. I'm even clear on what it takes to advance from Marketing Manager to Marketing Director and from Marketing Director to Vice President. But above those levels, what is required to get promoted from, say, Executive Vice President to *Senior* Executive Vice President?

In other words, at the most senior levels of the company, why do some leaders keep moving up the ladder and others don't?"

I've never forgotten what Mr. Pepper shared with me late that August evening. "Those who do not make it to the highest levels of the organization are the executives who stop being '*coachable*.' They believe they no longer need to accept feedback. They don't try to keep learning or growing, and they don't believe they need to stretch themselves anymore. They sit back, earn the big paycheck, and take in all the perks that come with a grand title. They believe they've 'made it.' Those are the leaders who don't last long because being coachable is fundamental to leadership success."

Mr. Pepper's powerful advice has influenced me ever since. Besides initiating a daily habit of asking myself, "How coachable am I today?" his words of wisdom factored into my decision to become an executive coach once I left the corporate world a few years later.

As a result of that encounter, a big part of what I do today is help executives make positive, forward-focused changes in their professional and personal lives. This allows them to advance in their careers through adapting their mindsets and their behaviors.

As you read this book, I encourage you to pause regularly and ask, "How coachable am I being right now?" If you disagree with the suggestions I've shared, I urge you to remember: A coachable leader—which means being a coachable *self*-leader—at least listens to suggestions before rejecting them.

To get the most out of Leading YOU™—and ultimately out of your career—I encourage you to stay open-minded to the ideas presented throughout. That's how you will break through the barriers that prevent you from reaching your full career potential.

What Do I Know About Coaching Executives, Anyway?

Before I began coaching senior execs, I spent 20 years in the corporate world, including several years as an executive myself, where I was responsible for leading dozens of brands across almost 50 countries and four continents. Now, well into the second decade of running my own business, I have had the honor of coaching 700+ executives representing more than 60 nationalities across six continents and more than 70 different industries. These experiences have given me an objective "armchair view" of what makes executives successful, as well as what causes them to derail their careers. Through these experiences, I've found out firsthand just how wise John Pepper's advice was so many years ago: Coachability does, indeed, make all the difference when it comes to driving greater leadership success in the workplace.

Yet, far too many gifted leaders are unaware of (or in denial of) the importance of coachability as it pertains to *self*-leadership. They find themselves stuck, wondering why they are stagnating in their careers. It isn't always a matter of ego; often, it's related to complacency, the result of becoming too comfortable, or a lack of self-awareness. They may simply not be tuned in to the absolute *need* to change. Like all of us, they could use a little nudge (or for some, a shove; for others, a full-body tackle) in order to see themselves as others do. Only then can they understand how their behaviors affect their outcomes at work.

Emerging Patterns

From the start of my executive coaching career, I saw distinct patterns emerging from the leaders I worked with. I saw executives from all corners of the globe repeating the same limiting behaviors over and over again (consciously or subconsciously). These behaviors were consistently stalling careers, but they weren't culturally driven, i.e., not by a uniquely "Western" or "Eastern" approach. In fact, I have witnessed the same damaging behaviors across dozens of geographic cultures.

In *Leading YOU*™, I'll point out the patterns, and then I'll share ways to shift those patterns so that you can strengthen your self-leadership and move forward in your career. Addressing these patterns directly will help you make it to the next level and gain all that comes with it—greater responsibility, heightened job satisfaction, a stronger sense of self, and more respect from others, as well as promotions, a higher salary, and larger bonuses.

Why Create an Executive Leadership Brand?

As the author of several books on both corporate and individual branding, it's no secret that I believe in the power of brands. Time and again, I've seen how branding can build stronger companies, catapult individual careers, and lead to increasingly greater achievements.

In my years as a brander and marketer in *Fortune* 100 companies, I witnessed this phenomenon firsthand. Since then, I have also seen it in my executive coaching practice, as well as when I speak at conventions and conduct leadership programs around the world. Yes, branding works for *everyone*—corporations, employees, first-time supervisors, middle managers, senior-level executives, board members, entrepreneurs, solo-preneurs, job seekers, and even graduates fresh out of university.

I consider this concept *especially* powerful for executives because every leader has a specific brand that affects his or her ability to lead effectively. It's what I call your Executive Leadership Brand—"The Trademarked YOU™®." Think of it this way: Nike and Starbucks have a "TM" after their name, so why shouldn't you? Place a ™ after your name, and think about what you want your Executive Leadership Brand to stand for.

Maybe you're resisting that advice or thinking, "Brenda, you've got me all wrong. I don't want or need a brand as a leader." Well, here's the deal: Whether you want a brand or not, you already have one. That's because I define your Executive Leadership Brand as *the way others perceive, think, and feel about you as an executive, compared with other leaders*. Since people at work already have perceptions, thoughts, and feelings about you, that means you are already branded as a leader, simply by virtue of being you in the workplace.

The question then becomes: As a leader in your organization, do you have the brand you *want*? If not, it's your responsibility to take charge of defining and communicating the leadership brand you desire. Because when it comes to branding yourself, there's one thing about which I am absolutely positive: How well you manage that brand makes all the difference in your success or failure. You don't want to leave it to chance.

Just as companies painstakingly define their brands and communicate them in the marketplace in order to better control how those brands are perceived by their target markets, so you, as a leader, can and should do the same in your workplace. Indeed, *unless you take control of your brand, your chances of making it to the upper echelons of any organization are limited.*

Branding Equals Big Egos, Right?

If you're still resistant to the concept of leadership branding, maybe you're thinking, "But, Brenda, people already accuse executives of having big egos. Why would I want to do something like create a brand for myself that would cause others to think I'm even *more* egotistical?"

That statement opens the door to one of the biggest myths about self-branding: that your brand is "all about you." Contrary to popular belief, developing an Executive Leadership Brand is not an ego exercise. In fact, because your brand is how *others* perceive, think, and feel about you, your brand's most important component isn't actually "you" at all. It's the "others" in your world who are doing the perceiving, the thinking, and the feeling. Without them, you can't even *have* a brand. It would be like the proverbial tree falling in the forest without anyone there to hear it.

So, while you absolutely do want to be authentic and not pretend to be someone you're not, you still have to get clear about how you come across to other people you work with. That requires regularly taking into account their perceptions.

Let me illustrate this by using the example of corporate brands. A corporate brand isn't really just about "the brand." It's about whether its target market will be interested in *buying* that brand. You can have the most revolutionary idea or product in the world, but if consumers perceive it as undesirable, you might as well close up shop. Similarly, if your Executive Leadership Brand is performing poorly, you won't reach your full potential.

If your Executive Leadership Brand is how you are perceived by *others,* what does self-leadership have to do with it? As I've said, it's only through mastery of *self-*leadership that you can truly lead others well. The 15 behaviors we explore in this book will help you to manage yourself more effectively so that you can be perceived as you desire—competent, confident, and authentic. So, even though self-leadership is all about you in terms of how you govern your own behaviors, it isn't all about you in the long run. Others will notice your self-leadership, and that will have a direct effect on your interactions with them.

Developing your Executive Leadership Brand requires knowing *what you want to stand for* as a leader and working consistently to communicate that brand effectively, while simultaneously taking key steps to avoid damaging it. A fundamental aspect of branding yourself is mastering self-leadership behaviors, and this book will help you do just that.

What is the "Experience" of Working With YOU™?

As a brand *passionista*, I enjoy finding analogies between corporate brands and individual leadership brands. With that in mind, here's a favorite that makes a strong case for having a powerful Executive Leadership Brand. (I doubt it will take you long to figure out which corporate brand I'm describing.)

If you had invested $10,000 in this company when it first went public in 1992, your investment would be worth more than $2,000,000 today, This brand currently has approximately 24,000 stores located in over 70 countries. If you haven't guessed it yet, this should help: Every morning, millions of people start their day by visiting one of this company's outlets for their favorite cup of java.[1]

Yes, indeed, it's Starbucks.[2]

Now, a lot (and I mean a *lot*) has been talked about, written about, and discussed about the Starbucks brand—and for good reason. Starbucks became the game-changer for the centuries-old, staid coffee industry. But what can Starbucks' branding success teach you about your own brand as a leader? What follows is an analogy originally based on a *Brandweek* magazine article (with updated statistics to reflect today's prices):

- Coffee, in its natural bean state, is a commodity that sells for about 3 to 5 cents per cup.
- Add packaging and a brand name to that coffee, place it on a grocery store shelf, and the price of that coffee rises to 10 to 50 cents per cup.
- That coffee, offered up with service and a smile (say, at a Dunkin' Donuts), increases the price to about $1-$2 per cup.
- Then, there's Starbucks, which sells its coffee worldwide for anywhere from $4 to $8 per cup.

Imagine—people flock there by the millions to spend *four times more* for a cup of coffee than anywhere else.

How does Starbucks get us to spend so much more of our hard-earned cash—and feel good about it while we're doing it? Because it offers its consumers so much more than just taste; it provides a *rewarding coffee experience*. At Starbucks, we're paying for the pleasure of taking a break during the day—watching the skilled baristas concoct our favorite

---

1. Starbucks Investor Relations, http://investor.starbucks.com/phoenix.zhtml?c=99518&p=irol-irhome.
2. Starbucks Coffee Information, International Stores, http://www.starbucks.com/business/international-stores.

choca-locca-mocha-frocha (I can never get those names right)—or enjoying a relaxing chat with friends after a night out.

That's what differentiates Starbucks from the dozens of other coffee brands out there and what has built such strong brand loyalty through the years, despite its higher price tag. So, what does this demonstrate?

People will pay more for a superior experience. Applying this truth to your own Executive Leadership Brand means that, if you want to earn more money, advance in your career, and rise to positions of greater responsibility, you must think about the *experience* YOU™ offer as a leader. And that experience will be greatly impacted by your self-leadership skills—no matter how much you believe you've developed your people-leadership skills.

That brings us to the key question: What is it like to work with you, honestly?

A couple of years ago when I was speaking at a conference on executive leadership branding, a Managing Director sat in the front row of the audience with his arms crossed and body slouched in his chair. His body language screamed, "I don't want to be here!"

A few minutes into my presentation, I shared the Starbucks analogy and asked the audience to consider the question, "Would YOU want to work with YOU? Think about it … what would that experience be like?"

A pregnant pause followed during which the Managing Director bolted straight up in his chair, and out of his mouth came the words, "Oh, sh**!" I doubt he intended to say that out loud, but the audience sure got a good chuckle out of it. For this particular individual, I think it was a "light bulb moment."

I have found that this powerful question stops people like a brick wall. We don't often think about ourselves from this perspective. But it's important to take the time to reflect on this question—and the questions that follow—and to be honest with yourself:

- What is the experience of working with you?
- What's it like to be your colleague? Your boss? A fellow board member?
- What's it like to be on the receiving end of what you deliver in the workplace?

Knowing your answers to these questions is fundamental to your success as a self-leader.

Break the "CCODE"

When I talk to clients about self-leadership, I like to use an acronym that spells out "CCODE" (yes, two C's) because I think it's the ideal recipe, both for being a savvy coaching client and for achieving success as a self-leader. The ingredients are as follows:

C is first for **Courage**. The first step in your evolution as a capable self-leader is taking a good, hard look at yourself—your work habits, your fears, your personal style, your relationships, where you thrive, and where you fall short. A true, no-holds-barred self-assessment takes guts. Confronting yourself and realizing that you have flaws that are holding you back can be painful. It takes courage to open your eyes, look in that mirror, and make changes that will have a powerful impact on your career.

C also stands for **Commitment**. Self-leadership isn't a goal to which you can aspire "a bit." It's like being a "little" ethical; you either are, or you aren't. Once you commit to being coachable—once you say you want to examine yourself and make whatever changes are necessary to be an effective self-leader—then you must devote yourself to the process, embrace it, and keep it at the top of your priority list. It deserves your time, focus, and attention.

O means you are **Open** to new ideas, new mindsets, and new ways of looking at your life, your work style, and your relationships. You're also open to changing the *way* you work. As I mentioned earlier, self-leaders are willing to at least listen to new ideas.

D is for **D**iscipline. This means putting systems in place and organizing yourself in a way that supports your progress. It involves arranging your schedule to find time for the changes you want to make. Disciplined self-leaders also make regular self-assessments a part of their routine so that they are continually checking progress and making adjustments.

E is for the Energy you must devote to this important mission. Don't underestimate the amount of energy you'll need to make changes in yourself. It amounts to conscientious self-care, and that's not something senior executives are always good at. It's too easy to blow off daily objectives like getting a good night's sleep, eating healthy foods, and fitting in regular exercise. But you cannot achieve your goals if your body and mind are tired. That's why this might be the most important **CCODE** component because, without healthy energy, the other objectives will be out of your reach.

Learn From the Mistakes of Others

Author John Luther Long once said, "Learn from the mistakes of others; you can never live long enough to make them all yourself." That's what this book will do for you—help you learn from the errors other leaders have made so that you don't have to make those same mistakes. I hope that you will take full advantage of that concept as you read *Leading YOU™*.

Please be prepared to:

- learn from the mistakes of others,
- challenge your assumptions,
- willingly change ingrained behaviors, and
- stay coachable.

By embracing that approach, you can master self-leadership and move forward in your career in a way that you've not been able to do before.

My Promise to You: I Won't Mince Words

At the beginning of any executive coaching engagement, I pose two questions:

1. "What do you want to achieve through the coaching process?"

2. "What kind of coach do you need me to be to help you succeed?"

While the answers to the first question vary dramatically, the answers to the second are almost always some version of, "Be a straight shooter!" "Don't hold back. Share with me your observations." "Hold up a mirror, and let me see all the warts."

So, just as I would in a live coaching session, I won't mince words in this book. I promise to challenge you. If what you read here goes against dearly held beliefs you have, you might find yourself getting riled up. If that's the case, and if what you read in these pages challenges your existing leadership paradigms, I encourage you to review the ideas presented with a curious and "coachable" attitude. Keeping an open mind just might lead to some surprising results for you and your career.

The Trap of "Authenticity"

As I said, you want to be authentic to who you are when defining your brand, but don't fall into the same trap as one of my clients. Donald was an executive at a multinational corporation who, frankly, had a terrible reputation within his company. When I conducted verbal feedback on Donald among his coworkers, the most consistent word used to describe him was "jerk." Clearly, working with Donald was not a "superior experience," and his Executive Leadership Brand was in serious trouble.

Perhaps someone like the infamous Steve Jobs could get away with being difficult, but most executives who behave this way are on the short road to damaging their careers. Donald's future opportunities were going to be severely limited unless he learned how to work more effectively with others.

Yet, when I addressed the issue with Donald, he made it clear that he was only willing to make a few changes in his behavior. "I do see that I need to make *some* changes," he told me, "but what I'm being asked to do is to be somebody I'm not." He dug in his heels and insisted that if he made the changes suggested by his feedback providers, he would be "inauthentic." His reasoning, essentially, echoed that old song, "I Gotta Be Me."

Unfortunately, this wasn't the first time I had observed a leader at work using "authenticity" as an excuse for treating others terribly, for lacking organization and time management, or for any number of other poor self-leadership behaviors.

So, I asked Donald to describe a "great" leader to me. Within minutes, he was able to make a long list of characteristics. The problem? He personally exhibited few of these traits. In fact, his behavior was often the direct opposite of what he knew an excellent leader to be—and all due to not addressing his own lack of self-leadership skills.

Donald then went on to say, "Actually, I can't think of a positive leadership role model I've had, so I don't really know what it means to be a 'good' self-leader. It's not my fault I'm bad at this!"

That's a fairly lame excuse. Think about it: Even if you've never had particularly great role models at work, I suspect that you could sit down with pen and paper and—within 20 seconds—make a long list of good self-leader characteristics. In fact, I'll bet the positive attributes would easily roll off the tip of your pen.

Go ahead and try it right now. Take a moment to write down the top words you believe describe a great self-leader. Here are some common characteristics that surface when I ask this question of my clients:

- Trustworthy, has integrity
- Adaptable
- Provides clarity
- Charismatic
- Only dives into details when necessary
- Not afraid of making tough decisions
- Courageous
- Transparent
- Approachable, open
- Good communicator
- Focused
- Level-headed

- Listens well
- Inspiring
- Optimistic
- Balanced risk-taker
- Takes blame where appropriate
- Balances short-term goals with long-term goals
- Shares praise
- Empathetic
- Emotionally intelligent
- Composed
- Keeps the big picture in mind

Now, sit back and look at each item on your list. Pick out the top attributes that you believe are the most important when it comes to truly excelling in self-leadership. On a scale from 1 to 10—with 1 being "Not like me at all," and 10 being "Very much like me"—how would you rank *yourself* for each of these characteristics right now? As always, be honest. Which characteristics would you have to develop the most to be the kind of coachable self-leader you would like to be?

Distinguishing the "What" From the "How"

Coming up with a list of desirable self-leadership traits—the "what" of how you want to be as a good leader—is the easy part. It's the "how" of it all, the *fulfilling* of those traits, that can be challenging.

And the reason why it's so difficult to achieve those traits may be because you've never really thought about or studied what it means to be a good self-leader. There's a good chance you've indulged in at least a few of the 15 behaviors I will share in this book—behaviors that can hold you back from reaching your full potential.

Leading YOU™ is filled with practical yet impactful "how to" strategies to help you eliminate these 15 potentially derailing behaviors. Once armed with this knowledge, you have the pathway to becoming a truly effective self-leader. That's when you will be fully ready to fast-track your own career and lead yourself and your organization to the kind of success you deserve.

2

Limiting Self-Leadership Behavior #1:
Believing You're a Victim at Work

I sensed Joseph's agitation the minute he arrived for his coaching session.

"You wouldn't believe the pressure I've been under," he said, "and it's all because of that jerk in the office across from mine!"

Joseph shared with me that he and his colleague, Eric—a fellow function head—had a combative relationship. Their one-on-one conversations always seemed to end up in an argument—a tale of two stubborn wills—and according to Joseph, Eric often undermined Joseph in meetings or in conversations with the CEO. As a result, Joseph felt he was looking like the weaker leader, which left him feeling defeated, tired, anxious, frustrated, and angry. "I'm telling you, Brenda, he's out to get me!"

The real problem behind this situation: In Joseph's mind, he wasn't in control—Eric was.

In my coaching practice, I've witnessed many leaders in a variety of posts who simply don't believe, deep down, that they are in control of their lives. They believe that colleagues, bosses, or "the system" are out to get them. As a result, they are quite often in a state of fear and distrust in the workplace. It's not necessarily a *conscious* state, but more of an underlying "hum" of subconscious fear that keeps leaders like Joseph feeling consistently anxious.

Since Joseph wasn't effectively managing his fear—nor the feeling that he was being threatened or manipulated by others—he wasn't effectively managing his self-leadership either.

But Isn't the Workplace Just Naturally Cut-Throat?

It may seem as though the work world is an environment where feeling like a victim is inevitable. After all, it can be competitive and judgmental, and it can seem like everybody is out for themselves as they compete for resources, business, accounts, and clients. Wall Street puts pressure on your organization to perform, and if you don't measure up, you're passed over for raises and promotions … or worse. How can you *not* feel victimized by all that?

The truth is that all of this behavior is *fear*-based. We're afraid of losing, of being judged, and of being shoved to the bottom. That can breed feelings of helplessness and the belief that we are at the mercy of others.

This is classic "victim mentality," and it causes you to believe that you don't have choices. But you absolutely *do*. You are not helpless nor are you "safer" if you feel like a victim. If anything, you're less safe because the choices you *do* make are likely to be knee-jerk, rather than made in a state of objective, calm confidence.

Thinking like a victim is actually not natural to us; it's a learned habit. From patterns picked up through life experiences, we learn to think in adversarial terms, and that tendency becomes heightened in competitive workplace environments. Chances are, many of your coworkers have a victim mentality, too. But I imagine you also know others who don't subscribe to the norm of victimhood. If so, those are most likely the individuals who have focused on and developed their self-leadership skills.

Strong self-leaders understand that it isn't necessary to give in to the culture of fear that's rampant in the work world. Those leaders recognize that we make our own opportunities.

In Joseph's case, perhaps Eric may have been trying to undermine him, or perhaps not. But the situation actually gave Joseph an opportunity to think differently, to rise up out of the drama and use his self-leadership skills to handle the conflict. When you stop playing the victim game, you automatically disarm those who you believed were "out to get you."

The truth is that *you* are creating your life, both at work and at home. Every minute, every hour, every day, you make choices—small and large decisions—and your resulting existence is the sum total of these. Put simply, your life reflects the choices you make. Clearly, then, the direction of your life is your responsibility, and no one else can *really* have the power to undermine you or cause you to feel threatened, diminished, or manipulated … unless you allow it.

Perception is Everything

Perception is everything in the world of branding, and it's also everything when it comes to victim mentality. When you let go of victimhood, you stop perceiving your experiences as negative. Instead, you see each circumstance in your life as an opportunity to learn, grow, and advance along the road of self-leadership mastery. Each situation represents a chance to make different choices.

As I reflect on my own life and career, I can honestly say that *everything* that has ever happened to me—which could have easily been perceived as negative—has eventually taught me something incredibly valuable. It isn't necessarily fun to get through tough situations, but as author Denis Waitley put it, "There are no mistakes or failures, only lessons."

Whenever something supposedly "bad" has occurred in my life, I sit back and ask myself, "What good will come out of this?" It may take a while, but eventually, I'm able to identify the benefit to what first appeared negative.

Here's a personal example: After a few years of working in the U.S., I reached a point where I had a strong desire to work overseas. I made it clear to my company several times that this was what I wanted. Finally, early one Monday morning, I was called into my boss's office where she shared the news: "You're moving to Prague!"

I was ecstatic! I bought every book I could find about the Czech Republic and read all about it. What a gorgeous city Prague was! Every book pointed to it as the best travel destination in Central and Eastern Europe. I was thrilled.

But the *following* Monday morning, I was called into my boss's office again. This time I was told, "Change of plans. You're moving to Warsaw, Poland instead." Now, no offense to Warsaw, but from the photos I had seen, it didn't look as nice as Prague. The sudden switch was an enormous blow to me. In the end, I did go ahead and agree to move to Poland, but I was admittedly not happy about it.

Now, when I look back on that decision, I have to laugh. Why? Because the decision to move to Warsaw was one of the best choices I ever made. You see, I moved there not long after the Berlin Wall had fallen, so Poland quickly became the powerhouse nucleus of Central and Eastern European business development—the most rapidly growing economy in the region.

Our company ballooned from 50 people when I arrived to more than 1,000 by the time I moved away just five years later. I was able to launch and grow a significant number of brands in a dynamic marketing environment that I would not have experienced in a smaller, less-growth-oriented country like the Czech Republic. All in all, it was an incredible time when my career flourished. And, on the personal front, I even met and married my husband while we were both expats living in Poland!

It just shows that what seems like something "bad" on the horizon may actually turn out to be a positive surprise—a fabulous episode in your life. In my experience, this has always been the case.

But if I had chosen to see that shift from Prague to Warsaw through the lens of a victim, believing that I had gotten the raw end of a tricky deal, I would have turned down the opportunity to work in Poland. I would not only have missed out on a thriving career, but I would not have met my husband.

I encourage my coaching clients to avoid thinking of events as either negative or positive. I ask them to view every situation objectively and celebrate the growth they have achieved as a result. In fact, right now, take a moment to think back on an incident or a time in your life when you feel you grew the most. My guess is that your progress came about because something challenged you—probably something you may have considered "bad" or felt frustrated about at the time.

The "You vs. Me" Mindset

One key to rejecting the victim mentality is to stop viewing others at work as if they are in opposition to you—no matter how they act. Remember that they may only be acting that way because they think you are in opposition to *them*. Bullying and harassment is often a reaction to victim thinking.

As soon as you view someone else as your adversary, you immediately create the potential for conflict, where one person has the power, and the other becomes the victim. Why is this non-productive?

- It's a "you vs. me" mentality, which is clearly not an inspiring form of self-leadership.

- It's a guaranteed way to damage your brand as a leader.

- It's the quickest way I've seen to demote yourself in the eyes of senior management, morphing you into "just another employee" with little or no authority.

How do you know if you're stuck in the "you vs. me" mentality? Here are a few "you vs. me" statements that can lower your status in your own self-leadership assessment, as well as in the minds of anyone who hears these comments.

- "Well, it's not my decision, but _____ says we have to …"
- "Believe me, I'm not any happier about this than you are, but here is what the senior management team is requiring us to do."
- "Why are my ideas constantly being shot down by top management? It's as if they don't trust me."

These types of comments weaken your self-leadership and can make you appear ineffective to others as well. Your language and behaviors should reflect your current position as an executive and key decision-maker—*and* the position you want next. So, if you've fallen prey to this pattern of verbal "victimhood," dig deep. A little voice inside you may be telling you that you aren't worthy of your current post or of working in a more senior position.

If that's true, the first step is to become aware of that mindset so that you can shift out of it and begin to develop genuine self-confidence in your ability as a leader. It's critical that you *believe* you not only deserve and are qualified for the position you have now, but that you are also ready for the next level in the company.

Fist Over Fist or Interlocked Hands—You Choose

Let me use a simple visual to symbolize this you-versus-me mindset that can easily keep you stuck in a victim mentality. Seeing it may help you avoid getting caught in this trap.

First, make a fist with each of your hands; then, place one vertically on top of the other so that the tops of the knuckles of both hands touch one another (just like the Fist Over Fist illustration on the next page). Now, think about it this way: The minute you complain about someone else impacting you somehow, you have become the bottom fist—the victim—while the person who has impacted you represents the fist that sits on top. As the lower fist, you're pushing upward against the top fist, and you will likely feel resistance, frustration, and anger. This hand configuration says, "I don't have control over what happens to me in my career, so I have to stay on the defensive, always watching out for someone who might undermine me."

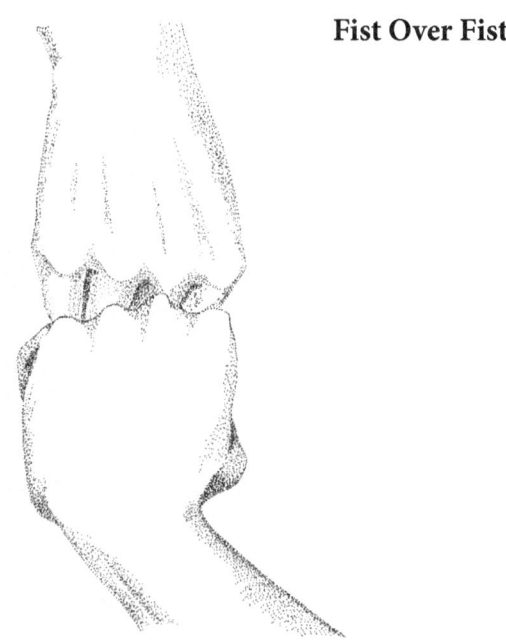

Fist Over Fist

Now, release your fists, and place your hands in front of you, side by side, with palms facing you and the fingers interlocked (as in the Interlocked Hands illustration on the next page). In that hand pose, you now demonstrate, "I play an equal part in this situation, working side by side with other leaders to find solutions to challenges."

I find this physical illustration to be a simple, yet powerful reminder of the choice you can make instead of being a victim. Keep this exercise in mind at all times. Whenever you find yourself feeling victimized in the workplace, interlock your hands (either physically or in your mind). Remember, as a strong self-leader, you don't want to place yourself in the position of being the bottom fist, constantly pushing against others.

Interlocked Hands

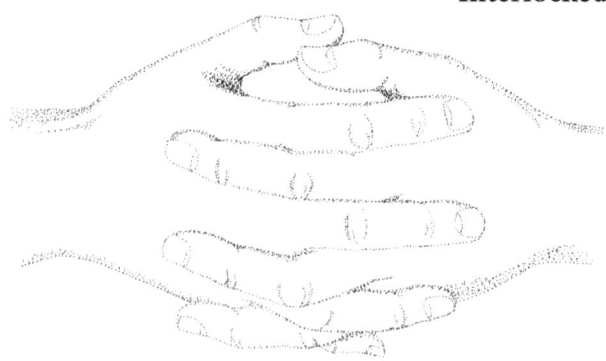

Instead, look at the situation through the eyes of the most senior leaders in your organization—the position where you *want* to be (if you're not already there)—and contemplate how to solve the problem instead of complaining about it. That's how you move yourself and the organization forward. Because the minute you take that objective, proactive view of yourself, you'll become more equal in your own eyes, as well as in the eyes of others—whether or not you've attained an official high-level title yet.

Putting the Interlocked Hands into Practice

What do you do if you believe upper management has made a poor decision—the kind you wouldn't want anybody else to think you support? Usually, I see leaders pursue one of four strategies when faced with such a situation or with any tough challenge at work: They cower, cope, conquer, or quit. Let me explain.

Cowering involves crouching down in fear and trying to hide from the problem. You hope it will just go away, but you still hold the problem front and center in your mind, which, of course, ensures that it *won't* go away. The outcome of this "strategy" is no resolution at all, while you continue to feel fearful and worried.

Coping involves learning to feel at peace with the decision and the outcomes. Essentially, if you can't come up with a better solution and you decide to cope, then don't complain. Nothing will weaken your Executive Leadership Brand faster than complaining about a situation that you have no idea how to solve. Instead, change your mind about the situation, and figure out a way to embrace the decision that has been made by upper management. Then, you'll be free to let go of feeling like a victim and will be able to move on. Bottom line: Pick your battles wisely.

What does *conquering* mean in this context? A conqueror steps in and takes on the challenge. Speak up calmly, rationally, and let your voice be heard by sharing your concerns with the person or people involved but not in a blaming or volatile way. Stick to the facts and/or rely on your experience. Then—and this is fundamental—offer a better solution. Remember, whatever your position in the organization, you're not paid to *complain* about problems; you are paid to *solve* them. If there's a conflict with a specific person, calmly and confidently offer to meet in the middle, and ask openly, "What would it take to make this work more effectively?"

Quitting isn't necessarily what it sounds like. Yes, you could definitely get so frustrated that you might give up and leave the organization altogether. That's an extreme reaction, though. Consider that option only if you truly cannot cope with what's happening.

Instead, what I mean by "quitting" is shutting down and avoiding the situation altogether. It isn't about "fearing" the issue—it's about completely checking out mentally. What effect does quitting have? It doesn't improve your self-leadership abilities, nor does it do anything for your organization. It's simply putting on blinders and walking away, postponing a decision or confrontation that you'll have to contend with eventually.

After reading these four scenarios, reflect on at least two times when you felt someone in your organization made a poor decision and there was a lot of disagreement among your colleagues about it. Which of the four behaviors did you choose in response: cower, cope, conquer, or quit? It's clear that cowering is never a good choice, and quitting isn't either, unless you feel the situation is so dire that you must genuinely leave your position and the company entirely. That's certainly a rare and drastic decision. Generally speaking, the best self-leaders opt to either cope or conquer, depending on the situation.

Whatever you do, avoid complaining about others or about "top management." Doing so is almost always a bad move that negatively affects your brand. It sends the wrong signals and paints you as a victim.

If you can adopt the habit of viewing life and your career as a series of learning experiences rather than feeling like a victim of "the next evil lurking around the corner," you'll stop worrying so much and be in a better space, both physically and mentally. You'll take on the challenges that come your way with confidence in your ability to overcome them. That's powerful self-leadership.

Limiting Self-Leadership Behavior #2:

Not Managing Your Mind

Victoria showed up at my office, looking forward to focusing on three behaviors that she had identified as holding her back in her career progression. Here's what she had written down:

1. I need to speak up more in meetings, particularly with senior leaders.

2. I need to stand up to pushy clients.

3. I need to become more comfortable promoting myself to top management.

But during our session together, it quickly became clear that the issue for Victoria wasn't necessarily these behaviors. Instead, it was her underlying *mind management* driving those limiting behaviors.

It isn't unusual for a potential coaching client to show up for a trial session with a change-in-behavior objective, and then realize that mind management is actually at the heart of the challenge.

In Victoria's case, through our discussion, she discovered that she had been quietly talking herself out of embracing the very behaviors she wanted to embody. She had been listening to that little voice inside her head that says, "If I speak up, I'll probably be wrong and make a fool of myself." Or: "Even if I don't agree, I don't want to rock the boat, so just go along with it." Or: "I've never been any good at self-promotion, so my chances of getting anywhere in this job are slim."

Does Victoria's dilemma ring true for you, too? These kinds of limiting thoughts can pass through your mind so quickly that you don't even consciously realize it. But these thoughts are incredibly powerful and can have a dramatic effect, causing you to postpone actions and make all sorts of excuses for not initiating positive change.

What's at the heart of it all? One of the worst enemies of self-leadership is a *fear of failure,* and it plagues even the most high-ranking executives. Here's another example: Sarah is a woman who helped start up a successful high-tech company. Previously a strong individual, full of energy and excitement, she and her fellow leaders grew the company from a dozen employees to a thriving organization of several hundred.

By that time, Sarah had become a mother, with one child already born and a second one on the way. She found herself struggling to balance the demands of work and home and realized that her family was getting the short end of the stick. So, after serious consideration, she decided to leave the work world for a few years to focus on raising her kids. Those "few years" turned into more than 10 years of being out of the corporate environment.

That's when Sarah arrived at my office for coaching. "I thought I could just pick up my career where I left off," she said, "but I realize I was being naïve. What was I thinking?"

She then proceeded to tell me about how she was certain she had completely blown her recent interview for a new position. "You won't believe what I said, Brenda," she told me. "What an idiot! How stupid can I be? Some of the answers I gave to questions were ridiculous, the more I think about them."

I looked at her and quickly changed my demeanor. "I can't believe you did that either, Sarah! What *were* you thinking? You really are an idiot, you know that? How stupid can you be! Your answers were completely ridiculous!"

Sarah looked at me with shock on her face, clearly taken aback by my words. But it only took her a moment to understand my purpose. When I saw the recognition register on her face, I returned to my normal tone of voice and asked, "Now, if I were your boss, Sarah, and I spoke to you that way, would you work for me?"

"No!" she said, "Of course, not! That would be the worst boss in the world!"

I responded, "But, all I did was mirror back to you exactly what you've been saying to yourself. My point is: You *have* been listening to the worst boss in the world—and it's that nasty little voice in your head."

The Power of That Nasty Little Voice

When it comes to mind management—a foundational element of self-leadership—it's absolutely critical to watch the little voice inside your head … like a *hawk*. Many executives deal with the same problem, so much so that author Seth Godin even wrote a blog post about this very issue called, "The World's Worst Boss."[3]

If you think about it, that inner voice is the one that talks to you the most (no matter how chatty your spouse or others in your life might be).

---

3. Godin, Seth, "The World's Worst Boss," *Seth's Blog,* http://sethgodin.typepad.com/seths_blog/2010/12/the-worlds-worst-boss.html.

So, it's fundamental to pay attention in order to get clear about what that voice is saying to you morning, noon, and night. Simply by paying attention, you can bring these thoughts to the surface and change the dialogue you have with yourself.

Remember: That voice has no right to treat you in a way that you wouldn't allow others to treat you. It's your choice which voice in your head you listen to—the one that tells you that you *are* ready to handle any job/challenge that comes your way … or the one that will defeat you.

Here's another example: Two clients of mine, Ravi and Samuel, were peers in the same bank and reported to the same boss. Neither of them knew I was coaching the other, of course, because the coaching relationship is confidential.

One day, Ravi called me, and I could tell from his voice that he was excited. "Brenda, guess what? I just found out that my boss is leaving the bank … and I want his job!"

"That's great," I responded. "I recommend you go to Human Resources and ask, 'What are the five key characteristics required for that position?' Then, let's meet up tomorrow morning and review those five characteristics together in order to get you ready to apply."

"Perfect," Ravi replied. "I'll see you tomorrow morning!" I hung up the phone.

Literally no more than five minutes later, Ravi's peer and colleague, Samuel, called me.

"Brenda, guess what?" Samuel asked. "I just found out that my boss is leaving the bank … and I want his job!"

"That's great," I responded the same way I had with Ravi. "I recommend you go to Human Resources, and ask, 'What are the five key characteristics required for that position?' Then, let's meet up tomorrow afternoon and review those five characteristics together in order to get you ready to apply."

"That sounds like a good plan," Samuel replied. "I'll see you tomorrow afternoon!"

The next morning, Ravi walked into my office, brimming with excitement. "I did what you suggested, Brenda, and I asked HR for the five characteristics they want in a candidate for my boss's job. Good news! *I have four of the five*, and I feel confident I can develop the fifth." So, Ravi and I spent the rest of that session helping him get prepared for how to position himself in a job interview, particularly when it came to that fifth "missing" characteristic.

That afternoon, Samuel arrived at my office. As he trudged in, I could immediately tell that his energy was low; he was sending signals that he felt down and defeated.

"Samuel, your energy seems to have shifted since we spoke yesterday," I said. "What happened?"

"You're right," he replied. "In fact, I almost cancelled this meeting. You see, I went to HR, just like we agreed, and I asked for the five characteristics they want in a candidate for my boss's job. But I've got bad news: *I only have four of the five*."

It was a classic example of how that little voice—the one that keeps resurrecting fear of failure—can mess with your mind to the point of derailing your career. The way Ravi and Samuel each viewed this challenge made all the difference in the outcome.

The "What You Think is What You Get" Triangle

Ravi and Samuel's different mindsets provide a perfect example for what I call the "What You Think is What You Get" Triangle ("WYTIWYG"). Starting from the bottom and working our way up, you can see the direct impact of each leader's belief.

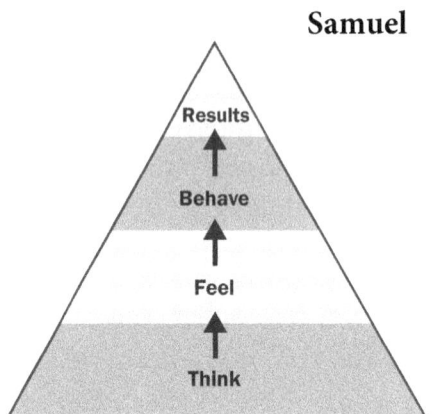

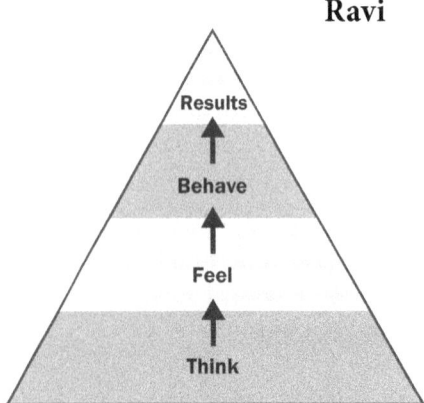

Let's begin with Samuel. His key thought was, "I only have four out of the five characteristics required." In other words, instead of seeing that he already had 80% of the traits needed, he chose to focus on the 20% that he lacked.

Working up through the model, that thought caused him to feel insecure and intimidated about his ability to succeed.

Now, keep in mind that anyone meeting Samuel would probably not be able to see his feelings of insecurity and intimidation. But working our way up the triangle, what *could* be seen was the behavior that resulted from how Samuel felt. And what was that behavior? He never even applied for the post. The outcome, then, is obvious: He didn't get the job.

In contrast, Ravi's key thought was, "Good news: I've got four of the five characteristics required!" So, working his way through the model, that thought made him feel confident that he could succeed. The behavior that resulted? He applied for the job and—you guessed it—he was the successful candidate.

I love this model because it's so incredibly simple, yet powerful: What you *think* drives how you *feel*; what you feel guides your *behavior;* and your behavior is what shapes the *outcomes* you get. It all starts with what you *think*. That's why it's so critical to tame and take charge of that little voice in your head.

How Does Your Own "What You Think is What You Get" Triangle Look?

Take a moment to reflect on a challenge you're facing right now. It can be personal, professional, related to your job, your family—whatever. Try walking through the triangle exercise from bottom to top, reflecting on the key thought that's related to your challenge. Then, ask yourself: "How does that specific thought make me feel? How does that feeling cause me to behave? What outcomes does that behavior bring?" All of these steps will ultimately affect your success and your brand as a self-leader.

Then, work your way through the triangle again, this time thinking a *positive, forward-focused* thought about that same challenge. What thought would you need to think to get a different outcome? Once you're clear on that, how does this new thought make you feel? How would that specific feeling make you behave? And what results would you get from that new behavior?

When it comes to self-leadership, you cannot underestimate the power of how you think. Simply adjusting your thoughts and feelings toward a situation can create a dramatic shift that drives positive, long-lasting change. That's the power of effective mind management.

Make a commitment to yourself that the next time a challenge arises, you'll remember to watch your thoughts carefully about that situation. Then, purposefully choose to think differently. You'll be amazed by how much this simple yet powerful mind management technique can quickly improve how you feel, the way you behave, and ultimately, the outcomes you achieve.

4

Limiting Self-Leadership Behavior #3:

Getting Stuck in Black-and-White Thinking

As Senior Director of Finance for a major insurance company, my client, Marilyn, knew more about rules and regulations than most of the people in her company. And she stuck to them—down to the tiniest detail. She acknowledged that she might be a bit rigid, but being flexible in her industry brought risks she just wasn't willing to take.

You see, over several years of working in such a highly regulated industry, Marilyn had learned the "right way" to do things, and once learned, she felt strongly that the company should stick to those "right ways." Given that she was also responsible for leading others, Marilyn was afraid to set a precedent by questioning a proven procedure or by doing anything substantially different from the past. She feared that her employees would get out of control and start bending the rules. "Color inside the lines," she told them. "That's how you avoid problems in this function and in this industry."

The higher Marilyn reached in the organization, however, the more this "black-and-white thinking" brought unexpected consequences. By the time I got involved with her as a coach, it had reached a point where Marilyn's colleagues wouldn't even approach her for opinions because she seemed unable or unwilling to offer useful, creative solutions. My verbal interviews with stakeholders revealed that, because of her rigidity around rules, she came across as cold and incapable of being collaborative.

Thus, Marilyn's colleagues were holding separate sidebar conversations. One by one, she watched other functional peers get promoted while she stayed at the same level.

Don't get me wrong—Marilyn was very good at what she did. She was reliable, incredibly knowledgeable, and she and her team produced good quality work. But based on my interviews, it was obvious to me that her attachment to black-and-white thinking was holding her back from moving forward in the organization. That's because, at the higher end of any organization, being strategically and executionally creative—even in a job as numbers-driven as finance—is critical to success.

Marilyn failed to realize that her ingrained belief in sticking to rules, which had served her well as a more junior leader, was now potentially sabotaging her ability to advance to more senior levels. She had gotten stuck in the fact that entry-level/junior positions in most professions are very often based on strict guidelines—what is right/wrong and good/bad.

It's true that early in your career, you have to learn the rules and work by them. But eventually, you do need to be confident enough to see smart ways to bend—or even change—those rules and to know *when* to bend or change them. In Marilyn's case, her growing organization needed a Finance Director who knew the rules well but who could also see the gray areas between black and white. Why? The higher up you get in an organization, the best solutions actually exist in the gray.

So, as you progress in any organization, the more important it is that you "get comfortable in the gray" in order to be ready to solve challenges with creative solutions. In other words, letting go of rigidity and assessing the subtleties of each situation are important aspects of self-leadership.

Why Do We Resort to Black-and-White Thinking?

Black-and-white thinking—defined as the ability to see one extreme or the other but not the space in between—is not that uncommon in the workplace. Why do we rely on it? There are many reasons.

First off, it's *easier*. If we pigeonhole people, problems, situations, and solutions based on the past, we never have to explore uncharted territory or admit that there may be a better way of doing something.

Aligning with what we believe are tried-and-true answers is *faster*, too. It takes extra time to look at new options and weigh pros and cons. And in today's 24-7 work world, getting problems off your desk and out of your mind in a speedy fashion can feel like a priority.

There is also a biological reason why we love black-and-white thinking. The brain—that small organ located in your head which only represents 2% of your body weight—uses a whopping 70% of the body's glucose, 25% of the body's oxygen, and 25% of its nutrients.[4]

As a result, the brain is always looking for ways to save energy, and black-and-white thinking is one such way. Simply put, making a decision based on how you've decided in the past *conserves energy*.

Safety is also a factor. Black-and-white thinking appears to involve fewer risks, and we feel more assured of success because the same old ways of doing things have worked before. But as we've seen with Marilyn, for senior leaders, the idea that it's safe to make the same decisions based on past experience is not only just plain false, but it's actually *riskier*.

---

4. "Human Brain Statistics," Statistic Brain via ScienceMaster.com, http://www.statisticbrain.com/human-brain-statistics/.

The Consequences of Inflexibility

Do you, like Marilyn, tend to stick to rules and procedures? Do you usually see things as right or wrong or good or bad, with little or no nuance? Perhaps you even consider this kind of rigidity to be one of your greatest strengths? If so, it may feel uncomfortable leaving behind the comfort zone of black-and-white thinking.

Here's a quick example of the downsides of not doing so: Within Marilyn's department, one of the financial analysts—who had worked there for eight years—suddenly became the caretaker for her ailing mother. The financial analyst took the initiative behind the scenes to figure out how she could both care for her mother and still accomplish her work. It would require some adjustments, though, such as working remotely part of the time and incorporating flex time into her schedule.

The analyst wasn't asking to reduce her hours or her workload, or to change any of her duties. She only needed approval to fulfill her family obligations in a different way. But policies such as flex time and working remotely hadn't been tried in Marilyn's area of the business yet. So, when the request surfaced on Marilyn's desk for approval, she said, "No." Marilyn was so concerned about setting a precedent that she became unwilling to even consider the possibility. Sadly, the very capable financial analyst left the insurance company to find more flexible work with one of the company's competitors.

I have seen many other situations where black-and-white thinking dramatically impacted people. For example, if a direct report has developed a performance problem, leaders may resort to the easiest, fastest "solution"—to terminate that person's employment—in order to avoid spending the time it would take to coach and help that person improve.

Let's face it: Life and work don't exist in black and white. Reality exists in a wide range of gray. This is especially true when you aspire to, or have reached, the higher ranks of an organization. Indeed, I can't think of a situation at that level in which the choices *don't* appear in varying degrees of grayness. For higher-level leadership positions, every choice includes variables that could affect success, and it can be enough to make your head spin. But achieving the best outcomes almost always depends on exploring those variables rather than quickly falling back on the tried-and-true, easiest option.

How do you begin to expand your thinking? As with all coaching, and as Marilyn learned, the first step is self-awareness.

How Do You Know if You're Operating in Black-and-White Mode?

In the interest of becoming more aware of your habits and thinking, let's find out if you, too, could benefit from becoming more flexible. Take this quiz to assess your own tendency toward black-and-white thinking.

Note: Respond "yes" if the answer holds true 50% of the time or more, and "no" if the answer holds true less than 50% of the time.

1. At the gut level, do you tend to judge decisions or people's actions immediately as either "right" or "wrong"? Yes___ No___

2. Do you quickly and instinctually look at situations that arise at work as either "good" or "bad"? Yes___ No___

3. Do you view other people or their choices as either "strong" or "weak," with no in-between? Yes___ No___

4. Do you find yourself labeling colleagues who agree with you as "smart" and those who disagree with you as "stupid" or at least "less competent"? Yes___ No___

5. Do you typically think in terms of either "success" or "failure," viewing failure as a catastrophic event? Yes___ No___

6. Do you rely primarily on previous experience to make judgments—not only about colleagues and their behaviors, but about whether a decision is right? Yes___ No___

7. Do you find yourself so pressed for time that you resort to quick choices based on what's been done in the past, without pausing to assess the specifics of the current situation? Yes___ No___

8. Do you find yourself frequently defending decisions by saying, "Well, that's the way it's been done before"? Yes___ No___

Now, add up the number of times you responded "yes." If you answered "yes" to only one or two questions, that can indicate you're reasonably flexible and seem comfortable working in the gray.

If you answered "yes" to three to five questions, you're spending some time in the gray but could definitely benefit from paying closer attention to situations where you fall back on black-and-white thinking.

If you answered "yes" to more than five questions, your self-leadership will improve immensely if you practice assessing each circumstance on its own merits, and avoid judging people or situations in black-and-white terms.

How Do You Let Go of Black-and-White Thinking?

If the quiz revealed in you a need to become less rigid (or if someone you know could benefit from these suggestions!), here are key strategies that you can use to increase your mental flexibility.

- Watch for a feeling of discomfort. What emotion rises up inside you when facing a situation which might be better served by exploring the gray? Being able to recognize when you need to set aside your usual way of thinking and be more flexible is key to taking that first step. If a situation isn't working out well, examine what's available in the gray areas outside of the status quo.

- When you find yourself judging someone as "strong," "weak," "stupid," or even "smart," remind yourself to ask why, and look at the situation again. Is your judgment really true? How do you *know* it to be true? Think about how you feel when someone else consistently labels you as either one way or another. It doesn't allow for the total expression of who you are, correct? Each of us can fall into any one of those definitions at different moments—strong, weak, smart, and less competent. Just like there is nothing all-or-nothing about you, remember that there is likewise nothing all-or-nothing about anyone else either.

- If someone makes a choice different from your own, check your value judgments, and ask yourself: What would prompt this person to make that choice? Avoid assuming that another way of doing things is necessarily inferior to your own approach. To avoid resorting to "right or wrong" thinking, inquire with genuine, open curiosity.

- Keep in mind: We all have failures as well as successes, and both are incredibly helpful. In fact, the most successful people usually fail the most because they did think in the gray and tried new approaches. That's why we have companies like Apple and many other successful start-up businesses. People who think in black-and-white terms tend to be more fearful of failure. It takes courage to go against the grain, and courage, in and of itself, is its own success, regardless of the ultimate outcome.

- Look at how other organizations are managing similar situations, learn about new technologies, and review research results in organizational dynamics. Take the time to learn something new! Here is where Marilyn was stuck, and if your own career is stalled, this may be the reason. As the late Dr. Wayne Dyer said, "Don't look back—that's not the direction you're going." Focus on the future and the promise it holds for you and your organization.

Learning to Thrive in the Gray

If you've ever read Victor Hugo's book, *Les Misérables*, or seen a film version of it, you know that Inspector Javert is a classic example of someone whose black-and-white thinking led to his ultimate demise. He had to see himself as good and right, and he had to see Jean Valjean as bad and wrong. So, when Valjean had the opportunity to kill the Inspector, but chose to spare his life instead, it was more than

Javert could bear. The world made no sense to him anymore because the gray was suddenly exposed to him—gray that he had previously refused to see. Faced with realizing he had walked his whole life with a wrong assumption about the world, Javert chose to take his own life. Ironically, of course, this was yet another example of black-and-white thinking—to live or not to live—instead of learning to get comfortable in the gray.

Even though black-and-white thinking in the work world is rarely that dramatic, numerous executives have come into my office on the way to the potential demise of their positions due to lack of flexibility in their thinking. Rigidity is simply dangerous on the job and in life. It's the height of refusing to be coachable.

We're creatures of habit, so the longer we stick to certain ways of being, thinking, and behaving, the harder it may seem to change. But that doesn't mean we can't. When was the last time you developed a new habit in place of an old one? I'll bet the result was positive.

Making a conscious effort to see the many shades of gray in any situation requires more of us. The key is to stay open to new modes of thinking. The world moves too quickly for any of us to stay stuck in patterns, simply relying on the way things used to be done. Given the speed of life today, I predict we will all have to reinvent ourselves many times during the course of our careers.

There is little to be gained from black-and-white thinking, but much to be gained from making the effort—and having the courage—to get out of the right-or-wrong world and live in the gray.

5

Limiting Self-Leadership Behavior #4:
Devoting Little or No Time to Strategic Thinking

My client, Myra, struggled with what I call the "Strategy vs. Execution Dilemma." She was a successful leader, in the running to become a Senior Vice President. She had gotten there by being known for *producing*, for always making sure that she and her team members were seen as delivering desired outcomes.

At the surface, this would seem like a good thing, right? So, you can imagine Myra's surprise when, during her performance review, her boss told her point-blank that the promotion she wanted so badly wasn't going to happen. The reason? Myra wasn't considered a *strategic thinker*. Ouch.

Myra immediately reached out to set up a coaching session. As she settled into the chair across from me, she admitted right up front that it was probably true. "Ever since my boss gave me the feedback, I've been thinking about what he said … and it's true. I do typically make sure the team and I are busy *doing* things, reaching our daily, weekly, and monthly objectives toward delivering our major projects. And that means I *do* spend the bulk of my time attending to details. That's been a good way to get where I am, but clearly, it isn't going to get me to where I want to go."

Upon further reflection, Myra shared that this tendency actually went way back. Getting things done efficiently and with excellence was how she impressed teachers as a student in school along with pretty much every boss she'd ever had. And she had always been rewarded well for her "get it done" behavior, too—earning good grades as a student and collecting raises and promotions throughout her career. Clearly and consistently, she proved that she was a go-getter and a producer.

But now, that seemingly positive behavior was holding her back. Indeed, while Myra and her team were delivering consistent excellence in execution, she wasn't doing the strategic work necessary to take her team, her function, and, therefore, the company to the next level.

Given her busy day-to-day world, it had never occurred to Myra that taking time to sit quietly and think strategically was actually what she was being *paid* to do. As a result, it now struck Myra that she was only doing part of her job—in short, she was *underperforming* as a leader by not taking regular time to focus on strategy.

For Myra, thinking strategically would represent a shift. It would take time away from attending to the day-to-day details of her workplace. It would mean sitting still, not visibly "doing" anything except thinking, reflecting, and challenging herself mentally. To Myra, who had been so busy all of her life and for whom the road to success had been paved with accolades related to her level of *activity*, this felt incredibly awkward, "wrong," and even "wasteful." She had fears of people judging her for laziness.

Can you relate to Myra's situation? If so, you're hardly alone. There seems to be an unspoken belief at work that just sitting and *thinking* is not a justifiable use of time. Some clients have told me that they feel so guilty if they aren't visibly "doing" something all of the time that they close the door or pull the shades in their office when they need to take time to think. They want to avoid being perceived as "not productive."

As children, we're often warned to stop "daydreaming"—both in school and at home. Our parents, teachers, and other authority figures didn't have much respect for staring out the window. Today, even though you are now in a higher-level position, that old conditioning may still be in your head, causing you to feel as though you're wasting time if you schedule "strategic thinking" in your calendar. But, like Myra, this belief might be holding you back from future career success.

When this self-awareness surfaced in our discussion, Myra's initial dismay and frustration turned to excitement as she began to contemplate the possibility of spending more of her time thinking strategically. But she wasn't sure what that would look like or how to go about doing it.

Before I tell you how Myra made the shift, and how you can, too, let's talk about how executives often get in their own way—even when they realize they *do* need to do more strategic thinking.

The Two Biggest Barriers to Strategic Thinking

Leaders who aren't accustomed to strategic thinking often assume that it will just magically "happen" once they get to a certain level or as soon as it becomes readily apparent that they need to do it. But I believe this shift actually requires specific, conscious changes regarding how you operate.

In my coaching practice, I have found that the main reason senior leaders ignore the importance of strategic thinking is that it calls for two things that typically seem to be in short supply: *(1) time,* and *(2) truly deep thinking.*

Far too many leaders (and companies in general) relegate strategic thinking to the once-a-year retreat where senior executives meet off-site somewhere, enjoy a few rounds of golf, participate in some team-building, knock down a few drinks, and talk about where the company should be in the next one, three, or five years. Then, they return to their crisis- and detail-filled days in the office, where they don't spend enough time or effort turning that strategy into reality.

Those periodic "strat plan" events are nice, but they don't reflect next-level thinking. When you postpone strategic thinking to a once-a-year event, you're not only thinking like a lower-level manager, but you're also not practicing good self-leadership.

Great self-leaders regularly take time for strategic thinking—not once a year, or even on an as-needed basis (e.g., when something big happens). It needs to be *ongoing*, even daily or weekly. In fact, for strong self-leaders, thinking strategically is literally a *way of being*.

How do you start? First, it requires shifting more and more responsibility to others who will attend to the details so that you can focus on the bigger picture. In short, if you want to grow in your career and rise to increasingly higher levels in your organization, the "doing" and the "thinking" aspects of your work must become more balanced.

How to Balance Thinking and Doing

Grab a piece of paper, draw a circle on it, and let it serve as a pie graph that represents 100% of your time. At the top, label it "Strategy vs. Execution."

Divide the graph into two pieces—one portion that reflects how much time you *currently* spend executing tasks and attending to details (execution/doing) and the other that reflects how much time you currently spend on thinking strategically (strategy/thinking). Be honest!

Label this circle "Current." If you're like many leaders I've worked with, your chart may reveal that you spend anywhere from 80-90% of your time executing, and only about 10-20% strategizing.

Next, underneath that same circle, draw a line, a colon, and another line that looks like this: _____ : _____ .

Let this represent the *optimal* ratio for these two aspects of self-leadership—how you probably *should* split your time between strategy and execution, given your current position. Is it 60% strategy/40% execution, 50:50, or something else? The best ratio for you will depend upon your organization and the expectations of your position (be sure to keep in mind the position you hope to achieve in the future, too).

Now that you've reflected on how much time you should be spending on strategy, it's time to make changes. I've found that the only way strategic thinking will "happen" in the middle of a busy week is for you to actually *make* it happen. How? Well, here's what Myra did: She started with reserving one hour for strategic thinking per week and increased those hours over time until she had reached her optimal ratio. As a result, her next performance review was much improved, and within a year, she was once again being considered for a Senior Vice President position.

Make a commitment to strategic thinking time, like Myra did: Shut your door and just *think*. To start, I suggest you begin with one hour, once or twice a week. Don't take calls during that reserved time, and don't be tempted to go to meetings. Just look at either your team, your function, or the entire company—as appropriate, given your position—and reflect on where and how your area or the company gets stuck, how to improve that and move forward, and how the company's progress and prosperity might change for the better as a result. Don't think about any details—*only strategy*. Decide that you'll set aside at least that much time every week, no matter what.

Wondering What to Strategize About?

This is a question I hear regularly: How do I know what I need to think about strategically? The answer is: All key issues need to be looked at strategically, particularly if you begin to see a pattern or a trend in the challenges that are arising in your work, your team's work, or an area of the company that impacts you.

Here's an example: Your direct reports consistently complain to you that people working in Operations aren't pulling their weight. Lower-level thinking would lead you to go to the head of Operations and say, "What's going on here? Shape up your team, would you?!" But that just leads to conflict and an unproductive "you vs. me" / "us vs. them" mindset.

Instead, every time a challenge rears its head, train your mind to automatically reflect: "Hmmm … this similar type of issue is being raised again and again. I wonder if there's a systemic problem somewhere." Once you've done that, you can then raise the issue up and above the "workplace level." Look at it from a higher place, and ask yourself questions such as:

1. Has this situation occurred multiple times and with the same players involved every time?

2. Is this just a one-time, specific situation, or is there a consistent underlying problem that can be resolved for a department, a division, or the entire organization?

3. Is the complaint or problem related to systems, processes, principles, or a values clash?

4. Explore deeper, and figure out if the issue has roots that reach into other departments or other situations. Connect the dots: A and B and C might appear separate and not linked to each other, but they may actually be connected if you rise out of your day-to-day thinking and look at them from a bird's-eye view. Is there some kind of relationship at play in the situation?

Looking at a problem in this way is what strategic thinking is all about: getting beyond the details of the complaints or challenges at hand, trying to detect a pattern, and seeing what could be adjusted to work better for the ultimate objectives of the organization. And it's a great demonstration of strong self-leadership.

A Case in Point

A few months ago, I dealt with a dynamic like point number 4 above. I was hired by a firm that provides professional services for many *Fortune* 500 companies. Their senior leaders were operating in silos, and the firm wanted to move forward as one, with all of the departments in concert with each other. But the head of Acquisitions and the head of Legal simply could not—*would* not (it's a choice, right?)—get along. No "kumbaya" here—these guys had a fierce and ongoing conflict.

On the surface, it's easy to think that this was just about two powerful leaders who disliked each other so much that they couldn't work together. But digging deeper revealed that the root problem was actually the way the firm had set up its KPIs—key performance indicators.

This company's leaders were rewarded, both financially and with recognition, for excelling *within their specific, individual areas.* As such, there were few structural benefits or incentives to help other leaders outside of their own departments. So ingrained was the current system of KPIs that the various division heads were not even encouraged to look beyond their own silos. There was no recognition system set up within the organization to encourage the type of collaboration that could grow or enhance the broader firm, as a whole.

I met with the division leaders and asked them to imagine they were looking down at the company from 35,000 feet in the air—far enough away that they could see the entire organization with all of its divisions and departments. They were to look for connections and walls, figuring out which departments stayed more isolated from the others, which walls were the thickest, and which communicated back and forth more easily. This mental exercise enabled them to *see the bigger picture,* a critical hallmark of higher-level, strategic thinking—and of self-leadership.

I then offered them another strategic-thinking exercise—to pretend they were totally objective consultants, highly paid and hired from outside their own organization, to come in and solve this challenge. From that viewpoint, what were the key strategic questions they would ask to help resolve these issues?

Once they identified the firm's KPIs as the central problem—a *systemic* issue—and looked at the firm from those two new perspectives, they could begin to piece together a solution. They were able to rise above what they had previously perceived as their personal dislikes and find a resolution that would benefit everyone involved: A portion of the year-end financial rewards would go to those who had clearly fostered collaboration between at least one or more departments or divisions.

Strategic Thinking is About "We," Not "Me"

In this type of problem-solving, there's no room for personalities, political maneuvering, or "he said/she said" comments. This is about *strategic thinking*, and that means focusing on the bigger "we," not the individual "you" or "me."

Just like getting out of black-and-white thinking and living in the gray requires more of you, so does strategic thinking. But this is where true higher-level growth comes in and allows you to use many more of your abilities at work.

Once consistently looking at the big picture becomes more natural for you, you'll be well on your way to higher levels of self-leadership and the benefits of more senior-level positions.

6

Limiting Self-Leadership Behavior #5:

Ignoring the Importance of Time Management

Billionaire John Paul Getty was a serial cigar smoker until he realized one day that—based on what he would earn hourly—he was spending the equivalent of $50,000 per year ... *smoking*. That wasn't $50,000 worth of cigars—it was $50,000 worth of his *time*. That kind of perspective definitely helps highlight the "time is money" concept, doesn't it?

Think about the words we use to speak about time. We *spend* it, *waste* it, and *save* it—just like money. We put a premium on it. If you thought of every minute of your day as being worth, say, $1,000, wouldn't you look at that minute differently? Once you appreciate the true "value" of your time, you'll *spend* it more wisely, *waste* less of it, and *save* yourself a lot more as well.

Another phrase I often hear is, "I will *make time* in my calendar for ..." But, let's face it: There are only 24 hours in a day. You cannot physically "make" more time unless you invent a time machine. (And if you figure that one out, I'd like to invest.) But even though you cannot create more time, you *can* use your time more productively and prioritize your time better. The strongest self-leaders have learned how to do that because they realize how vital it is to becoming a successful executive.

Now, if you groan at the thought of discussing "time management," I understand. We've all heard that phrase ad nauseam. But despite all of the talk, as I see it, we haven't gotten noticeably better at it. In fact, with the onslaught of constant attention-grabbers like email on smart phones, social media, and apps, the challenge has actually gotten worse, leaving us to ask the question: How do you find *time* for time management?

This issue comes up repeatedly with new coaching clients who complain that they're working longer hours than ever, but still not completing their highest-priority tasks. And to make matters more complicated, corporations continue to expand globally at an unprecedented pace, requiring leaders to take on new responsibilities that span continents or, at a minimum, to work with colleagues in multiple time zones. That leaves them juggling workloads and further fueling a "24-7-365" mentality.

A work day that often starts with a 6:00 a.m. conference call with someone on one continent halfway around the world may end with an 11:00 p.m. conference call with someone else on another. And what's the outcome? High stress—both physical and mental—and a work/life balance that's completely off-kilter, causing personal pressures *outside* of work as well. (Is your spouse unhappy because you don't spend enough time with family? If so, there's a sizeable club you can join.)

When asked, these leaders recognize that they are practicing anything *but* good self-leadership. Yet, I often hear, "It's not my fault, Brenda; it really *is* out of my control."

But is it? I have watched coaching clients become amazing time managers in remarkably short periods of time. They learn to balance where they spend their time, both at work and at home, so that they do more of *what* they want *when* they want. It's a matter of realizing what's holding them back and what's within their power to change. And if they can do it, so can you.

Control the Clock—Not the Other Way Around

You really *can* control the clock rather than fall victim to it. In fact, your ability or inability to take control of your time can make or break your career. So, if you find yourself frequently falling behind in your tasks, even though you work 10, 12, 14, or even 16 hours a day, it's a sign that your self-leadership skills in this area could use a boost.

How do you go about regaining control of your time? The first step is to find out the truth about what you do every day. That's why I ask coaching clients who are struggling with time management to create a log that's laid out in 15-minute increments from the moment they wake up until the time they go to bed—for 14 straight days (including weekends). You may be resistant to this exercise, but trust me: It's the #1 way I've seen clients put a stop to long work hours.

For this exercise, you can track how you spend your time in a table format, or you can create a form in Excel—whatever works for you. The key is to be methodical and disciplined, consistently carrying the log around with you and remembering to jot down what you are *honestly* doing during each 15-minute segment of the day. Start on a Monday morning of a two-week period that you expect will be somewhat typical of your normal schedule, and do this for the entire two weeks through the end of the second Sunday. (If you feel you can only do this for one week, then keep your log from a Monday to the following Sunday; however, I do encourage you to complete two full weeks, if possible. The more data you have to analyze, the better.)

The key to a successful log is not to "judge" what you write down—just be completely honest. Pretend you're an anthropologist, just looking objectively at what's going on in your life, and record it without adjusting or filtering or assessing it. And in your descriptions of how you are using your time, it's important to be as specific as possible. That will help later on.

Here's a sample log from a client who was based in Asia:

From	To	Activity
05:45	06:00	Check and respond to emails received overnight
06:00	06:15	Check and respond to emails received overnight
06:15	06:30	Take a shower
06:30	06:45	Get dressed
07:00	07:15	Listen to the news, read newspaper, eat breakfast
07:15	07:30	Listen to the news, read newspaper, eat breakfast
07:30	07:45	Drive kids to school
...	...	...
11:30	11:45	Check emails
11:45	12:00	Conversation with Jan about XYZ Project
12:00	12:15	Conversation with Jan about XYZ Project
12:15	12:30	Lunch at desk
12:30	12:45	Check emails
12:45	13:00	Prep for 1 p.m. meeting
13:00	13:15	Operations Leadership Team Meeting
13:15	13:30	Operations Leadership Team Meeting
...	...	...
20:00	20:15	Watch TV
20:15	20:30	Watch TV
20:30	20:45	Get kids ready for bed
20:45	21:00	Talk with spouse about kids' tuition
21:00	21:15	Call with Michel in Paris about ABC Project
21:15	21:30	Call with Michel in Paris about ABC Project
21:30	21:45	Catch up on reading for work
...	...	...
23:45	24:00	Get ready for bed
24:00		Sleep

After two weeks of diligently keeping your time log, print it all out, then buy some colored highlighters. Sit down with the printout, and highlight the entries by different colors, line by line, per the color code as outlined on the next page. (If your log is in Excel, you can use the highlighter function to fill in cells with different colors.)

If an entry pertains to …	Then mark it …
Travel	Blue
Examples include: commuting to and from the office, travel time on planes, taking a taxi from the airport to a hotel	
Emails/administration	Purple
Examples include: checking and responding to emails, opening snail mail, completing your expense report	
Meetings/work calls	Yellow
Examples include: attending business meetings, talking on the phone to colleagues to discuss a project, doing a remote-employee's annual review over VOIP, sitting with your personal assistant to organize your calendar	
Private work time	Orange
Examples include: reading work articles and reports by yourself, completing key work-related tasks on your own, personal focus time to prepare for an upcoming presentation you will give, thinking strategically on your own	
Personal/self-care	Green
Examples include: relaxing, sleeping, eating, showering, attending yoga class, going to the gym, watching television/a movie	
Personal/family	Gray
Examples include: spending time with your spouse, taking your kids to soccer practice, attending a dinner with extended family, taking your aging mother to her doctor's appointment	
Personal/social	Pink
Examples include: attending a party with friends, having dinner with your spouse and another couple, going to a sports bar to watch a game with your university buddies	
Personal/self-development	White
Examples include: reading a self-help book, reading the newspaper to get up to date on the world, attending a course in person or online, attending a professional development seminar	

Feel free to add your own categories, as appropriate. For example, some of my clients spend a fair amount of time volunteering, so they have added a "Volunteering" category to their logs.

Is Your Time Being Well-Spent?

When you're done, sit back and look at your log. It will give you a much clearer "snapshot" of how and where you spend your time, but don't get specific yet about *what* you did during each 15-minute segment. Instead, hang the entire two-week analysis on the wall, stand back, and look at it: Which color sticks out the most? What is the second most frequent color? The third? Which colors appear *least*?

If you've never logged your time so precisely before, this exercise can be a real eye-opener. There are 168 hours in every week, and you may be quite surprised to discover how many of those hours are spent on activities that you actually don't want to do or that you consider less than productive. Again, the key is not to judge. For now, you're just objectively exploring.

Take a few minutes to reflect:

- What did you learn from keeping track of how you spend your time?

- What new patterns did you uncover?

- What pleases you most about what you see in your analysis? Where are you spending the "right amount" of time, in your opinion?

- Being honest, which aspects are you unhappy about and would like to change? Where are you spending too much or too little time?

Some clients like to calculate the percentage of time they are spending in each of their categories and make a pie graph of the results. Then—and here's the important part—they create a *new* pie graph that reflects the percentages of how they *want* to spend their time—the ideal pie chart percentages they want to achieve.

Whether or not you create your own pie graph, ask yourself these questions: How can you use the outcomes of this exercise to your advantage? What changes do you want to make? Then, set a plan in motion to focus your time where you want to spend it most and least, and outline the specific changes you want to make in your schedule—all guided by your commitment to stronger self-leadership.

The Biggest Time-Wasters

In my experience reviewing hundreds of time logs, there are consistently two major culprits that cause the most time management issues: attending meetings, and writing/responding to emails. Does this sound familiar to you, too? Let's explore each of these, one at a time.

#1 Time-Waster: Meetings that Hijack Your Time. A survey conducted among 2,000 British employees highlighted that the average UK worker will attend 6,239 meetings during his/her career.[5] Is that just a "British thing?" Not according to the time logs of my clients, who hail from over 60 nationalities and 70 industries.

The number of meetings held daily at any given company is staggering. And since senior leaders seem to be invited to the bulk of those meetings—and often feel obliged to attend—the victim mentality frequently kicks in when I discuss this topic. "But I *have* to go to that meeting. I don't have a choice," I hear leaders say. This, in spite of the fact that a whopping 60% of the people in that same British survey said they find meetings "pretty pointless."

If attending meetings is one of your biggest time-robbers, too, never fear. There *is* something you can do about it. Remember when I asked you to consider how you would look at your time if you knew every

---

5. "Had a meeting? Just 6,239 to go! Survey finds how average British worker sits through thousands of work meetings in their lifetimes," *Daily Mail*, Published April 1, 2015, http://www.dailymail.co.uk/news/article-3022047/Had-meeting-Just-6-239-Survey-finds-average-British-worker-sits-thousands-work-meetings-lifetimes.html#ixzz4HMkCM4Fj.

minute was worth $1,000? Well, this holds particularly true for time spent in meetings.

As a coach, I'm often asked to "shadow" executives in their workplace, frequently in meetings. I sit there quietly observing so that I can provide feedback later on what I saw and heard. As I look around those meeting rooms, I sometimes pause to consider the amount of total salary that's being spent by the organization to have all of those individuals in the same room at the same time. Can you imagine?

If this is true for you, or if you find yourself in a meeting that doesn't truly require your presence, pause and reflect: You may actually be doing a *disservice* to your organization by attending that meeting. Think about it: Every minute you spend during work hours is a company asset. Just like you wouldn't misuse a company car or waste office equipment or materials, so you shouldn't waste your limited time in meetings that don't honestly need your talents and attention. Your duty is to use your time—the company's asset—in the most effective way possible.

How to Use Your Time Wisely? Choose Your Meetings Wisely

The key is to get real about which meetings you honestly *do* and *do not* need to attend. That means saying "yes" only to meeting invitations where your presence is absolutely required and you can add value. How can you tell if a meeting is necessary or if it's going to be a time-waster?

First, ask for an agenda in advance that clearly states the purpose/objective of the meeting. Once you get the agenda, here are some tips to determine if your attendance is truly required, as well as ways to say "no," how to handle difficult meetings, and how to effectively plan your own meetings.

- Will it truly benefit the *company* if you attend? If so, how?
- Will it benefit *you as a leader* if you attend? Perhaps the meeting is to cover a topic you know little about, but you'd like to improve

your understanding. Or perhaps it's a meeting that will be attended by much higher senior-level leaders, and you want to observe how they conduct themselves. Just be careful not to go simply because the information is "intriguing" rather than useful. And remember: If you attend, you should plan to contribute.

- Would attending the meeting be a possible means for you to strengthen important relationships, either with a particular person or with a specific group of people?

- Is it truly necessary for *you* to be there, or could you ask someone else to attend in your place? For example, could this meeting be a good learning and development opportunity for one of your direct reports? Would someone else be more qualified or better able to contribute to the meeting than you? If so, share your thoughts in advance with that person as a pre-brief for your replacement.

- Do you need to attend the entire meeting or, after review of the agenda, is there only a portion of the meeting that's truly relevant to you? This is a consistent problem shared by many of my clients. They sit through an entire 3-hour meeting even though they were only needed for, say, 30 minutes. They might spend the remainder of the meeting checking email on their phones, all the while resenting the waste of their time. In fact, in the survey I mentioned of British employees, one in five adults admitted to sleeping during a work meeting, and 70% confessed that they frequently "zone out" during meetings. Whether you fall asleep or not, if your body language screams that you don't want to be there, it could do more damage to your brand than not. So, if need be, let the meeting planner know you'll attend only for the specific time related to a particular topic.

- Could you attend the meeting via video or by phone? Just be careful: It's easy to get distracted with other tasks, such as emails, when you aren't physically present at a meeting. I'll share in a moment how your brain cannot truly "multi-task." For now, rest in the knowledge that research reveals it's better to be truly *present* during a meeting, even if only for a short period of time.

- Let's say you've reviewed the agenda and have determined that it really *isn't* necessary for you to attend, neither for the company nor for you personally. How do you get out of attending the meeting gracefully and still preserve positive relationships with the organizers? Sometimes, you simply have to say "no" with calm confidence. Let the meeting planner know that you appreciate being invited but that you feel your attendance isn't necessary. Then, offer to read a summary of the meeting and follow up with any comments you might have.

- What happens if you're in a meeting that's being poorly run? Make a calm but firm suggestion: "We seem to be getting off topic. How can we get back on track?"

- What if you are in a meeting that's running overtime? Opt to excuse yourself by saying something like, "I have to stick to schedule and leave, but please do send me the meeting summary. Thank you."

- For any meetings you decide to attend, schedule a 10-15 minute buffer before and after. Use the time before the meeting to ask yourself: What is the objective of this meeting? Why am I attending? What do I personally want to achieve by attending? What does success look like for me at the end of the meeting? Then, after the meeting, ask yourself: What were the one, two, or three key takeaways from that meeting? What are the implications for my team or function? What are the next steps I've committed to, if any, and who needs to be aware of them?

- How about when it's your turn to call a meeting? Pause, and ask yourself: How will this meeting truly add value for me, my team, the people I'm inviting, and for the company? Be respectful of others' time, and whenever possible, cut down on the number of gatherings by streamlining and combining topics.

- Here's yet another category of meetings that is very important to schedule, but often overlooked: frequent meetings with *yourself*. Every week, carve out specific focus times to accomplish your own work. Guard those times carefully, and make it clear to the coworkers impacted that you won't answer calls or set up meetings during those periods. Ask your assistant to help claim that time for you, too, letting others know that, unless it's a true emergency, you want no interruptions. There is no need to be apologetic about it; just be direct. Doing this helps you avoid the constant interruptions that add to your days and that can prevent you from finishing your most important tasks. Ultimately, you'll perform better as a self-leader if you claim this well-deserved "self-time."

Using the guidelines outlined, how many meetings could you eliminate from your schedule in order to free up valuable time?

#2 Time-Waster: Emails—The Constant Interruption. Since our phones and computers typically make a sound or vibrate every time we get an email, it can be tempting to interrupt what we're doing to take a look. But unless you're waiting for specific important inbox material, this is a major distraction and time-waster. Each time you interrupt your concentration, you have to take a few seconds or even minutes to regain the same level of focus on what you were doing before.

The idea that we can "multi-task" is a myth. Indeed, researchers have demonstrated that our brains are simply not capable of doing two things at once. All we can truly do is what is called "rapid refocus"—quickly shift from one focal point to another—and doing so not only wastes time, but tires the brain, too. The outcome? We are more likely to make mistakes and be burnt out at the end of the day.

Here are two tips to prevent emails from distracting you and robbing you of so much time:

- Just like the recommended "meeting for yourself," dedicate focused time for reading, writing, and responding to emails. Give yourself specific guidelines for email management, and stick to them. For example, let your staff know that you'll be working on email without interruption from, say, 8:30-9:15 every morning and from 3:00-4:00 every afternoon. If you plan for this focus and make it an ongoing habit, you'll be amazed by how much you can accomplish.

- Get voice-activated software, and dictate your emails by voice instead of typing them. Despite the fact that I type faster than 100 words per minute, my productivity virtually doubles when I dictate emails into my computer rather than type them. I use software called Dragon Naturally Speaking, but there are other brands of voice-activated software to choose from, too. Be sure to program it to understand your accent and your specific enunciation patterns. Once you do, you may become addicted to it like I am, especially if you aren't a particularly speedy typist. I've seen this type of software save hours per week for many of my coaching clients.

Tips for Creating a "Time Savings Plan"

Now that you have a better idea of where you are wasting time, let's look at some ways to help you *save* time and put it in your "bank."

1. *Set priorities, and guard them vehemently.* When someone requests your help for something, take a moment to reflect, "If I do this, will it take time away from my key priorities for the day?" If so, ask if you could help later. If you want to practice excellent time management, learning to say "no" comfortably is key. Don't allow anything or anyone to take you away from your priorities unless the situation absolutely cannot wait. (If saying "no" is a challenge for you, don't worry. We'll get to that in the next chapter.)

2. *Understand your biorhythms.* Whenever you feel your energy is either high or low, record the times of day in a notebook or an Excel sheet. Do this for a week or two, and you'll most likely begin to see patterns. These are your biorhythms, and being aware of these personal energy peaks and troughs throughout the day will allow you to plan your work on top priorities—or even to plan important meetings—during the times of day when you have the most energy. Likewise, you can plan breaks at times when your energy typically slumps. This will help lower your fatigue at the end of the day, too, because you won't be trying to push yourself to do tasks while your body is resisting.

3. ***Delegate, delegate, delegate.*** Upon closer scrutiny, most of my clients find that they can delegate many tasks on their plate. What is on your to-do list that someone else could conceivably do? More importantly, how could you turn those tasks or projects into great development opportunities for your direct reports? Smart delegation takes practice, but it will give you back more time than just about any other tactic. (If delegation is a particular problem for you, I dedicated an entire chapter to this topic in the companion to this book, *Would YOU Want to Work for YOU™? How to Build an Executive Leadership Brand that Inspires Loyalty and Drives Employee Performance.*)

4. ***Install a big clock on your wall.*** Time can slip right by if you don't stay aware of how much passes while you are working on a task. Keep an eye on the clock to make sure you aren't devoting too much time to lesser priorities. The last thing you want is to spend two hours answering unnecessary emails when you really need to be preparing an important report. Set an alarm to go off when you want to be finished with a certain task and start on another. This can help discipline you to stick to your schedule.

5. ***At the end of each day, write down the top three priorities you want to achieve during the following day.*** Then, when you arrive in the morning, do nothing else until you've accomplished at least one of those top priorities. By doing so, you'll start the day with a sense of accomplishment that will help fuel you to finish your other key tasks. Be ruthless about your top priorities—like a dog with a bone! I've seen this single habit transform dozens of leaders' effectiveness and help them become dramatically more productive.

6. ***Make use of idle time.*** One of my clients set up a regular weekly phone meeting with her remotely located division head during her 20-minute morning car ride to the office. She saw it as a great way to use that time when she would otherwise just be sitting and staring through the windshield. How can *you* use time wisely when you are waiting somewhere or stuck in traffic? Think about your regular activities. When do you have idle time, and what

could you do to make it productive? By the way, this may mean you use this "idle" time to relax, which is certainly justifiable, if you need more rest. Just make sure that you use the time to truly relax, clear your mind, and refresh your body—don't do something unproductive that prevents you from actually de-stressing, like watching YouTube videos or playing a game on your smart phone.

7. ***Create a to-do list, listing the tasks by order of importance.*** Then, stick to working on those tasks in that order, from most important to least important. Most people create to-do lists in random order and jump to the easiest or least painful tasks first, postponing the ones they don't want to do until later. But often, the tasks they don't want to do—or that are the most challenging—are the most crucial tasks to be accomplished. Then, before they know it, the day is over, and they're stuck at the office until 9:00 p.m. or later, trying to finish what has to get done. The longer you put off an unpleasant task, the longer you live with the stress of anticipating it. If you focus on the most important tasks first, you can let that stress go for the remainder of the day. Also, don't forget that if you put off doing your most important tasks until later, you're likely to run out of the good mental energy needed to accomplish what is most critical.

Put One Foot In Front of the Other

Hopefully, by now, you have a much clearer idea of your time-wasting practices. So, how do you begin to create new time-management habits? Start small. Instilling a new habit is much less intimidating if you don't require too much of yourself in the beginning. As you experience success, you can add additional, incremental steps to your overall goal. Once you begin to see the great results you've gotten from just a little bit of effort, you'll be pleasantly surprised to find more new and unexpected ways appearing that can help you make positive time-management change.

Adopting new habits can be an investment at first, taking a bit more time in the beginning and requiring energy, concentration, and determination. But the fact is, your investment will pay back many times over in the long-run. The process can take as much or as little time as you want, depending on how determined you are. But hundreds of clients have demonstrated that it absolutely, positively can be done! A full and balanced life—with time for work, time for family, and time for play—is definitely within your grasp. The bottom line is, once again, self-leadership.

A Bonus for YOU™

For more insights into how to take back control of your time, listen to the recording of New Zealand's "time queen" radio host, Robyn Pearce, as she interviews me about time management.

www.BrendaBence.com/TimeManagementInterview

7

Limiting Self-Leadership Behavior #6:

Saying "Yes" When You Want to Say "No"

If you're like most busy executives, your day may go something like this: Headquarters wants your profit projections for next quarter a week in advance of when you and your team had planned. There's a line of direct reports outside your office door waiting to meet with you, your inbox is filled with 300+ unanswered emails, and you haven't yet prepared the keynote speech you are giving tonight at a charity dinner. Meanwhile, your son needs help with his math homework, your spouse complains because you haven't been home for dinner in a week, and your ailing parents' financial situation needs your attention.

It's enough to make anyone feel dizzy and stressed out. And the truth is, something has to give if you don't want to crack under the pressure. But the question is: *What?*

When I say "something has to give," what I really mean is that you need to say "no" to some of these pressures. And in order to do that, you must draw strength from your self-leadership bank. As we began to address in the last chapter, learning how and when to say "no"—unapologetically and without guilt—is fundamental to leadership success.

You don't want to turn away from the people who need you—neither at work nor in your personal life—but that doesn't mean you need to become a pushover either. For many leaders, it means learning to avoid being so "nice" that you overextend yourself.

Saying "yes" to too much causes physical and emotional stress, can damage relationships, and can leave very little time for self-care. That can result in rising blood pressure, poor health in general, and may cause you to fall ill. It's a vicious cycle if you don't put a stop to it.

Being in charge of when you say "yes" and when you say "no" is key to taking control of your life. Saying "no" in a calm, comfortable, and collected way becomes more and more critical as you take on increasingly high levels of responsibility.

Why Do We Say "Yes" When We Really Want To Say "No"?

If you are like most executives I have worked with, you've said "yes" when you really wanted to say "no" more times than you care to remember. The truth is: We've all fallen into that trap. Why do we do it? Here are a few of the most common reasons I've uncovered when discussing this phenomenon with coaching clients:

- We fear conflict. We don't want the other person to feel disappointed or become upset. We don't want to create any ill will in the workplace, and we don't want to appear lazy.

- We have the misguided notion that we can "do it all." No matter how many times we've fallen short, we still manage to convince ourselves that there are more hours in a day than 24. If we just work a bit faster or push ourselves a bit harder, we believe we can keep everybody happy.

- It can be difficult because of cultural norms or because our parents raised us to be helpful to others at all costs.

Whatever the reason, the consequences of not learning how to say "no" can harm more than just your health. It can actually *damage* more relationships than it preserves. You may end up making mistakes or failing to notice something important at work—an error that could have serious consequences for you, your team, your boss, or the organization as a whole. You might also lose your cool and find yourself getting angry at the very people who have asked something of you. But, of course, if you've agreed to do what they asked, it isn't their fault. It's your own responsibility to say "no."

Let's face it: When you have more plates in the air than you can possibly keep spinning, some of them are going to fall and break, and someone's needs end up being sacrificed. (It's often those of your spouse, your kids—or yourself.) It's time to curb this "saying yes" habit—one of the keys to effective self-leadership.

Yes, You Can Learn to Say "No"

If saying "no" is difficult for you—whether it's always challenging or only in certain circumstances—you can make it easier by following some key steps:

1. *Get clear on how your life would be better if you didn't have so much on your plate.* How would your life be different if you could learn to say "no" effectively? Make the longest list possible of all the benefits of saying "no." For example, your list might include: (a) less stress, (b) more time to spend with your family, and (c) fewer feelings of resentment toward the people who expect so much of you. Keep writing until you've uncovered all of the possible upsides of saying "no."

2. *Accept that you do need to get better at saying "no."* Sit back and make an honest assessment of your workload. How many tasks or activities have you taken on because you didn't say "no"? Review your to-do's, and put a checkmark next to each task or activity that you would honestly like to cross off. What issues are you encountering due to having said "yes" to these tasks?

3. *Recognize opportunities to say "no."* A keen awareness of a problem is the key to changing it. For a week or two, take note of all the times when you could have said "no" but chose to say "yes." What drove those decisions? Note the times when it felt right to say "yes," and those when it didn't. What would have happened if you had said "no," and what are the consequences you fear in each situation if you *were* to say "no"? Assessing these opportunities will help you sort out what's most important and which fears are stopping you from saying "no" when that's what you really want.

4. *Begin by saying "no" to smaller requests.* A sympathetic yet firm "I'm not able to do that right now" works well. If you're asked why, simply reply that it's conflicting with key priorities that must be done first for both you and your team. Most reasonable people will accept this as an adequate response. Remember, too, that you can say "no" to things that aren't direct requests, such as someone who walks into your office and expects you to drop what you're doing to talk with them. All that is required is a simple response, such as, "Thanks for stopping by. Right now, I'm focusing on a key priority. When might be a good time to talk about this later?"

   Are you unsure if you should say "yes" or "no" to a request? Then, the best choice is to avoid committing in the moment, either way. You might say, "Let me think about that, and I'll get back to you by 4:00 p.m." Then, take the time to reflect—without the pressure of someone standing there—to determine if saying "yes" is really the right thing to do.

5. *Practice saying "no"—literally.* If saying "no" is a particular problem for you, practice it in front of the mirror or on an audio recording. Remember: You want to sound assertive rather than unsure or angry. Watch yourself in the mirror, and listen to your voice. Do you look and sound as if you mean it, without apology or guilt? Or do you look or sound angry or aggressive? If so, your anger may be because you've put yourself out too much already. It may also be because you feel the need to be forceful in order to be heard, which often comes from a deep-seated feeling of guilt about turning down requests. Remind yourself that you have every right

to say "no," and say it calmly and confidently. If you say it with aggression or anger, you're almost certain to cause ill will between you and the person making the request.

6. ***Stick to your convictions.*** If someone tries to convince you to change your "no" into a "yes," ask that person to respect your decision as final. Don't offer reasons for saying "no" unless you really believe doing so will defuse a potentially explosive situation, or if you feel the individual making the request deserves to hear your reasons.

   Most of the time, however, you don't owe anyone excuses or reasons why you need to say "no." An exception to that rule: If you're saying "no" to your boss, of course, it's smart to offer clear reasons why you believe you can't take on a new task. (In Chapter 10, we'll talk about how to "manage up" effectively.) If you *do* offer reasons, be succinct, calm, and confident. Going on and on with multiple reasons could actually make you sound guilty and defensive.

7. ***Watch your body language.*** If your mouth is saying "no," but your body language is saying, "I'm not sure," you'll have an executive brand buster on your hands. To make sure your body is helping you stick to your convictions, turn full-face to the person you are addressing, and maintain an open, confident stance. Avoid crossing your arms protectively or looking away when you say "no." If you are standing, avoid shifting from one foot to the other. Whether you are standing or sitting, be sure to maintain eye contact with the person.

8. ***Take note of what it's like to say "no" to the little things.*** After each positive experience of saying "no," sit back and assess. What did you experience? Relief? Self-confidence? Pride in your ability to push back? Or did you feel discomfort and guilt? If so, keep practicing. Eventually, it will get easier for you. Recognize and reward yourself for each successful "no."

9. ***Make saying "no" a regular habit.*** After some practice, you'll find yourself able to say "no" to increasingly bigger requests. You'll be able to discern quickly when you want to avoid something and

when you're happy to say "yes." Check back with the "benefits" list you made in Step 1 to remind yourself of the impact this skill will have on the overall quality of your life. Saying "no" will soon become commonplace for you.

You may never be completely rid of your guilt feelings or discomfort when you have to say "no" to someone. But over time, you won't be as affected by it. Remember: You're not a bad person because you don't say "yes" to everything that's asked of you. You will actually do less good for others if you haven't done what's right for *you* first before attending to others' needs. That's just one more benefit of successfully mastering the art of saying "no."

Saying "No" with Tact and Respect

Of course, it isn't just *saying* "no" that matters; it's *how* you say "no" that's key. Remember, you're becoming an expert at leading *yourself*, and that means mastering your emotions and behaviors in awkward and difficult situations. Saying "no" is the perfect opportunity to practice tact and respect, even when you think the person in front of you is being unreasonable. If you can say "no" to that person diplomatically and respectfully, you will have mastered a key self-leadership skill. We've touched on this subject a bit; here are a few more pointers to help you say "no" skillfully.

1. ***Listen to the request in full, without interruption.*** It's much easier for people to receive a negative response if they feel their request has first been listened to and carefully considered.

2. ***Seek to clarify before responding.*** Before you answer, ask open-ended questions, as necessary, to make sure you fully understand the request. Be specific, and avoid questions that will give you no more information than "yes" or "no." For example, you might ask: "How much of a time commitment do you expect you would need from me for this? What is your deadline for this task?"

3. ***Avoid over-apologizing.*** Remind yourself that you have every right to say "no," so avoid apologizing. However, if you do feel

strongly that you need to apologize for not being able to help, then only apologize once. Phrases like, "I'm really, really sorry about this," or "I feel so badly about this," will actually make you sound like a poor self-leader.

4. *Don't leave people hanging.* If you have to turn someone down, do it reasonably quickly after the initial request. Don't leave them wondering what your answer will be; that just causes angst. And when you're boosting your own self-leadership skills, the last thing you want is to procrastinate and allow potentially difficult situations to build up.

The Most Common—and Damaging—Example of Not Saying "No"

I couldn't possibly count the number of times a coaching client has said to me, "I get no 'real' vacation time because I'm always in contact with the office, even when I'm with my family." It's the most common example I hear of executives not saying "no" when doing so would make a significant difference to their well-being.

Do any of these scenarios sound familiar to you?

- You choose your vacation hotel or resort because it has a strong wireless connection that will allow you to easily email documents to the office and have VOIP calls without interruption.

- The plane lands at your holiday destination, and immediately upon turning on your smart phone, you see 14 missed calls from work.

- You miss breakfast with your family because you're busy putting out fires via email at the start of your day.

- Your spouse is upset because you take calls while at the beach, at dinner, at the museum … pretty much everywhere you go during your so-called vacation.

- You have to leave your family and return to your hotel room for a Skype call with your boss.

- You find yourself more stressed *after* your holiday than you were before you left because you spent your time away trying to juggle work and leisure.

In these days of inexpensive and easy connections by email, mobile phone, and video conferencing, your holiday location can easily become more of a temporary office in a faraway destination, rather than true "time off."

While on vacation, do your team, peers, colleagues, and boss expect you to be "with them" 24/7, putting out fires, participating in important decisions, and advising them on how to handle issues? If so, remember that when you let them draw you back into "the office" while you're away, self-leadership falls by the wayside.

The Vacation Solution

The first step in solving this problem is to think about what really prevents you from totally disconnecting from the office while you're away. Is it that you don't trust your colleagues to do a good job while you're gone? Is it that you secretly don't *want* them to survive—let alone thrive—without you, so you can prove you're irreplaceable? These are tough questions to ask yourself, but taking the time to reflect on your answers will have a big impact on the outcomes.

Take some time to examine your thoughts about being gone from the office. Smart leaders know that when their organization, division, or department runs smoothly during their absence, it's actually a sign of excellent management on their part. If things go well while you're gone, it doesn't make you unimportant. It simply means that you have trained your team and/or the people you work with well enough to handle situations so that you can afford to be on vacation for a while. If you have the luxury of time, they can still hold off making the most important decisions upon your return.

For a lot of leaders, the constant interruptions while on holiday are simply a result of not having established clear enough boundaries up front. After all, other people will assume that you're fine with the interruptions unless you tell them otherwise! If you haven't pushed back on this before, why would they think you have an issue with it now? Essentially, through your past willingness to accept work calls and interruptions while on vacation, you have "trained" others to believe it's acceptable.

What can you do to retrain yourself and others so that you can enjoy your breaks in peace? Here are some tips:

- **Notify people.** Many weeks in advance, tell everyone—at work and in your personal life—the dates when you will be gone. Put it in your electronic calendar so that others can see those dates as reserved. Make sure they're clear about your intention to "divorce" yourself from work during that time.

- **Enlist help.** Get everyone involved in helping you lay the groundwork for some true downtime, and won't you be surprised when they actually enjoy the assignment? Ask them to become part of the solution, not the problem, and you'll likely find more support than you expected.

  For example, you could ask a member of your team to take over a particular project and only contact you in the event of a dire emergency. Your assistant could field your phone calls with a script such as, "Actually, he's out of the office right now and can't be reached until February 12th. I'm happy to take a message and have him return your call when he's back." If the party presses your assistant, the script could continue as, "He's not reachable until that date, but perhaps someone else could help you in the meantime?"

- **Anticipate.** Think about the activities and projects your colleagues and direct reports will be involved in while you're away, and prepare everyone who needs to know about them. Ask them to think proactively about any issues that might arise while you are gone so that you can address any problems *before* you leave.

- **Set clear expectations up front.** One week before you depart for your holiday, send a notice to everyone you think appropriate, setting guidelines about how you will be managing communications while you're gone. For instance, you can let them know that you'll be checking emails once every four days (or perhaps not at all), and ask people to refrain from sending you "nice-to-know" emails. If they feel they must, you can suggest they write "Nice to Know" in the subject line. That way, you can de-prioritize those emails when you are "triaging" your inbox upon return.

- **Don't forget to "manage up."** Alert your boss or the Executive Committee that you will leave matters in your coworkers'/direct reports' hands while you're gone. Lay down your boundaries with them as well, so that you can wholly claim your well-deserved downtime.

Great Self-Leaders Have Clear Priorities

Learning to say "no" when it's appropriate strengthens your self-leadership. It shows that you're a decisive person with clear priorities, and you know how to plan your time effectively. You take on what you can conceivably do well without adding so much to your schedule that you're unable to produce good quality work.

With all of this in mind, learning to say "no" can actually be one of the best things you can do for yourself, for your team, and for those you love. It reduces stress and gives you back time for what—and who—is most important in your life.

8

Limiting Self-Leadership Behavior #7:
Failing to Address Conflict When It Arises

My client, Sonya, was head of the Operations function in her organization when her boss was struck with a severe illness that forced him to suddenly quit his job. As a result, Sonya was catapulted overnight to the role of General Manager. She went from being peers with her fellow function heads to becoming their boss. And some of them weren't exactly happy about that.

To make the situation more challenging, Sonya had been raised in an Asian culture where harmony is a critical value and a key to success in work and life. On the other hand, the function heads now reporting to her came from mixed backgrounds, but quite a few from Western cultures. Harmony wasn't a key value for them, so her leadership meetings were a struggle from the start, with considerable conflict and all sorts of games being played.

Because of Sonya's desire to maintain a pleasant environment and make sure people were happy, her efforts at placating everyone didn't resolve issues. In fact, some of her team members didn't take her seriously, and the tensions between them persisted. She came to me in a state of desperation, needing help to find a solution.

I had a hunch that Sonya might benefit from exploring her mindset around conflict. So, the first thing we did was use the "What You Think is What You Get Triangle" that I introduced in Chapter 2, starting from the bottom and working our way up.

Current

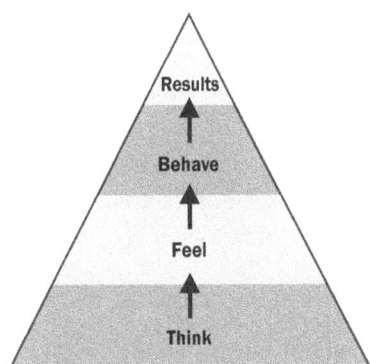

I don't resolve issues, and the leadership team ends up not being aligned.
I gloss over it when someone objects to something I say or do. I just turn away from dissent, or I agree with that person, even if I don't *really* agree.
Nervous. When someone disagrees with me or starts an argument with me, my mind gets garbled, and I don't think clearly.
"Conflicts are bad, so I avoid them as much as possible."

First, I asked Sonya to tell me her main thought about conflict. Her answer was steeped in her experience and the way she was raised: "Conflicts are bad, so I avoid them as much as possible."

Next, I asked her how that thought made her *feel* about arguments when they did happen. Sonya said, "Nervous. When someone disagrees with me or starts an argument with me, my mind gets garbled, and I don't think clearly."

Moving up the triangle, I asked, "So, when you feel nervous, how does that make you *behave*? What are the actions you take or the reactions you have as a result of that feeling?"

"I gloss over it when someone objects to something I say or do. I just turn away from dissent, or I agree with that person, even if I don't *really* agree," she answered.

Lastly, I asked her what the outcomes were of simply ignoring disagreements. "I don't resolve issues," she said, "and the leadership team ends up not being aligned."

Through doing this exercise, Sonya began to realize that it was *her own thinking* and the resulting behaviors she exhibited—not the actions of her colleagues—that were actually keeping conflict alive.

We tend to think of conflict as problems with "other" people, and we look for ways to change *their* behavior. But managing conflict is largely an "inside job," a matter of self-leadership. Sure, your negotiating skills and everything else you've learned about working with others will come into play, but your self-leadership skills will set both a tone and an example. The better you manage *yourself*, the better each conflict that arises will be managed overall.

When I asked Sonya to reflect on the overall impact of her behavior on her individual brand as a leader, she admitted it probably made her appear ineffective and that conflict management was an area she could definitely work on as a way to strengthen her self-leadership.

Why Arguing Can Be a Good Thing

Regardless of the culture we come from, let's face it: Few of us actually *enjoy* arguments. They can be unpleasant and give us anxiety because, if they escalate, we might damage a relationship or create bad feelings that linger. Once people feel hurt or insulted, it isn't always easy to regain their trust or respect.

But that doesn't mean conflict is always a bad thing. The truth is, arguments are a natural and unavoidable part of work life. Leaders who avoid them do so at their peril. Indeed, as long as we don't let arguments get out of hand and turn into useless shouting matches, they actually have a number of advantages.

Arguments allow ...

- people to participate in discussions;
- new ideas and perspectives to surface;
- improvement, forward movement, and positive change rather than stagnation; and
- a clearing of the air so that issues don't fester.

A modern-day example of how arguments can bring about positive outcomes is the relationship between Bill Gates and Steve Jobs. They had a famous, history-making argument that led them to launch two separate companies. Without that argument, we might not have the products we use every day from Microsoft and Apple.

If you tend to avoid arguments (and many of us do), try on the WYTIWYG Triangle yourself. Start at the bottom and work through the Triangle, asking yourself what you honestly *think* about arguments, how that specific thought makes you *feel*, how that feeling in turn influences your *behaviors*, and what the *outcomes* are of those behaviors. In short, reflect on how those behaviors impact your brand as a leader. Then, you'll see how that single, foundational *thought* that you have around conflict ultimately impacts the results you get.

Once done, redo your triangle, this time thinking a *productive* thought about arguments, how that thought would make you feel, how that feeling would make you behave, and the results that you would get from that new behavior. It's a powerful shift.

Here's how that second triangle turned out for Sonya: In order to alter her results, we went back to the beginning and considered how the outcome would change if she modified the way she thought about conflict, keeping in mind that *what you think is what you get.*

This time, when I asked Sonya to come up with a constructive thought about conflict to replace her prior negative thought, she said, "Conflict is actually *good.* It leads to positive and productive outcomes."

Future

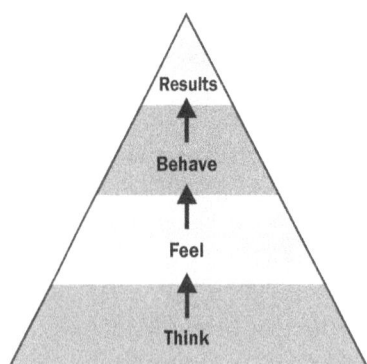

Results	The dissenting person would feel acknowledged, the meeting would carry on, and everyone would benefit from new ideas being shared.
Behave	Acknowledge the person's point of view instead of trying to avoid it. Seek to understand before judging.
Feel	I would feel appreciative of the person arguing, and I would respect the value they added to the conversation.
Think	"Conflict is actually *good*. It leads to positive and productive outcomes."

"OK," I said. "Now, how would that thought make you feel when you are in a situation involving conflict?"

She reflected for a moment before speaking. "I would feel appreciative of the person arguing, and I would respect the value they added to the conversation."

We continued on to reveal that this feeling, in turn, would cause Sonya to behave differently from before. She would acknowledge the person's point of view instead of trying to avoid it. She would seek to understand before judging.

The ultimate result? The dissenting person would feel acknowledged, the meeting would carry on, and everyone would benefit from new ideas being shared.

Through this exercise, by simply changing the way Sonya *thought* about conflict—which in turn would shift her feelings and behaviors about conflict—she could immediately get better results. In other words, by practicing good self-leadership whenever tensions arose, Sonya would strengthen her leadership brand.

Make a commitment to yourself that the next time a conflict or argument arises in the workplace, you'll *think differently* about that conflict in order to get better outcomes.

The Five Levels of Focus

A while back, I was coaching Robert, a division leader who worked for a large conglomerate. Like Sonya, he complained about a lot of infighting, power plays, and jockeying for position among the various division heads—meaning, between Robert and his peers.

In this case, functional silos had been built up for years. These individuals fiercely protected their own territories and wouldn't think of looking outside their areas to see how they might help strengthen other divisions. It had reached a point where these silos were bringing down the entire organization, trickling down to the lower ranks and making the company less successful, less forward-looking, and in the end, overall less competitive and profitable. My client wanted to see this conflict resolved, but he was at a loss as to how he could stop the dysfunction and start the healing.

When I met with Robert, I shared a model called "The Five Levels of Focus." Created by Australian author and consultant David Rock, the model suggests that, at any point in time, we all have one of five levels where we can choose to focus our energy and attention. Applying the Five Levels of Focus can help leaders deal better with conflict at work. For explanation purposes, let's start at the bottom and move around the five levels.

> 5. **Drama.** How do you know if you are (or someone else is) in the middle of "Drama?" You'll hear phrases like, "Joe told me that the R&D team is not on track to meet the deadline for the XYZ project!" or "I heard the accounting department has so many issues that everybody there is talking about resigning!" or "Operations and Marketing apparently don't get along at all, and everyone says that's what's slowing down the new product launch."
>
> Drama is akin to gossip, and it serves no constructive purpose. In fact, Drama exists primarily in the past, which means it cannot be changed. Focusing on what you cannot change wastes time, energy, and resources, and it certainly doesn't demonstrate good self-leadership.

Yet, the siren song of Drama can be mighty alluring, sucking you into its vortex like a vacuum. Similar to running on a hamster wheel, Drama won't get you anywhere, but it can be hard to stop once it gets going. It's surprising how many executives get embroiled in Drama (consciously or subconsciously), spinning their wheels, only to feel immense frustration when they and their teams aren't progressing forward.

How do you know if someone is perpetuating Drama in the workplace? They give negative feedback about a task that was done incorrectly in the past and/or create a culture in which blame gets tossed around freely. Here are a few additional behaviors that can indicate leaders are operating at the Drama level:

- They seek attention.
- They tell long "he said/she said" stories with lots of detail.
- They lower their voices or even whisper to add excitement and intrigue to their tales.
- Their self-worth comes from "being in the know" about other peoples' challenges and issues.
- They gossip, either passing on stories they've heard or creating content for gossip themselves.
- They're vocally critical of the system and others.
- They have a tendency to whine and/or exaggerate.
- They can easily become defensive, emotional, irrational, and/or upset.
- They're self-focused/self-involved.

Leaders who create these types of environments often get stuck in Drama by habit and don't—or can't—move until they recognize it and make a conscious effort to lift themselves out of it.

If you're stuck in Drama, your brand may unwittingly become "the person who complains a lot." Poor managers might even unknowingly reward this behavior based on the "squeaky wheel gets the grease" syndrome, but there's no question that an image of "Drama-creator" is not the kind of self-leadership image you want to cultivate.

4. **Problems.** Perched just one step above the level of Drama is "Problems." Concentrating on Problems is another poor self-leadership behavior in which you spend time focusing on what's going *wrong*. If you hear yourself bringing up the past or remaining in the Problems of the present, the aura around you will be negative, and you'll struggle to move toward solutions.

   You can recognize if you're at the Problems level because you'll tend to say things like, "I can't believe this project is falling behind," or "None of you are doing this right," or "Of course, you know who's going to be blamed for this!"

   Here are a few more indications that you're focusing on Problems:

   - You dive deeply into learning all of the details of what has gone wrong.

   - You find yourself returning to a problem again and again.

   - You have to admit that a part of you enjoys the adrenaline rush of wallowing in the problem.

   - You micro-manage and accuse others of doing things incorrectly.

   - You find yourself becoming defensive if someone brings up a problem.

   - People often describe you as "negative" or "unhappy."

   - As soon as you solve one problem, you're likely to find—or even create—a new one.

   As a leader, if you need to discuss a problem, it should be only for the purpose of illuminating a forward-thinking strategy to resolve the problem, not for pointing fingers. Forward-thinking focus is where great self-leaders place their energy.

That leads us to the top of the model, to Vision.

1. **Vision.** Vision is about *what* is to be accomplished, so this level is where great self-leaders spend the bulk of their mental energy. Vision centers on the promise of the future. It answers the questions, "Where are we headed as an organization/a team? How does what you're talking about right now relate to where we want to go?"

   The best leaders are able to identify when they or others are in Drama and Problems and, more importantly, they know how to guide themselves up into Vision.

   Here are some indicators to help you know if/when you are in the Vision level of focus:

   - You're passionate about the future because you know what it will bring; you've seen it and experienced it in your mind's eye.
   - You exude inherent optimism when talking about the Vision.
   - You're forward-thinking and focused on possibilities, not limitations.
   - You're centered and calm, no matter what seeming crises arise.
   - You promote ideas, helping others see and embrace the Vision.
   - You drive everyone toward greater opportunities.
   - You tend to be creative and experimental, willing to take risks.
   - Because you aren't mired in the details, you can easily connect the dots and see a bigger picture to come.

2. **Planning.** This level, situated just below Vision, has to do with *how* a company's/leader's Vision will be accomplished, so it's also centered on the promise of the future. If Vision is "what" the future holds, Planning is "how" it will happen. Planning answers the question, "What steps will we take to get to where we want to go?"

Focusing on this level gets people to roll up their sleeves and work toward achieving the desired result.

Here are some indicators of how to identify if you are working at the Planning level:

- You spend time thinking about structures, systems, and processes.

- You're confident and action-oriented because you have a clear plan to follow.

- You often work closely with others because you know working together is critical to making plans come to life.

- You can easily identify and preempt problems or risks because you're always thinking ahead to the next step.

- You're motivated and inspiring because you're on a mission.

- You remain composed because you know exactly where you need to go.

- You have a can-do attitude and consistently help others find creative ways of working around obstacles and roadblocks.

When you're focused on the Planning and Vision levels, you spend time on the goals you want to achieve. You put in motion the steps that will help you and your team achieve your Vision. This is what moves you, your function, and the entire organization ahead, and that's what great self-leaders do.

3. **Details.** Effective self-leaders spend most of their time "soaring" at the Vision and Planning levels, focusing on the "what" and the "how" of achieving the Vision. So, when should a great self-leader focus on Details? Only when necessary and only enough to glean the information needed. On occasion, you may need to swoop down and check out Details. The key is not to stay there for long but to soar back up to the Vision and Planning levels as quickly as possible, once you have the details you need.

When you spend too much time in the Details, you tend to take two different approaches, which are both counterproductive. If you're too embroiled at this level, you may find yourself …

- *Getting "lost" in Details,* asking too many questions, appearing impatient, and jumping too far into the minutiae. If you focus too much on Details, you can easily get off track.

- *Getting "seduced" by Details,* similar to a trivia game, asking questions about *interesting* data rather than truly *useful* information. Great self-leaders only deal with the necessary Details that will help them make plans to achieve their Vision.

The most effective leaders swoop down just long enough to take a look at the necessary Details, and then quickly soar back up to Vision and Planning. And any time someone tries to drive a great self-leader down into Drama and Problems, that leader immediately finds a way to remain at the productive and forward-focused Vision and Planning levels.

For example, let's say that you're in a meeting with some peers, and suddenly, you realize that everyone is diving into the Details of a particularly tough issue (adding a little Drama and Problems here and there). You stop, pause for a moment, and ask your colleagues, "How does this situation relate to our Vision for this year and the goals that we've set for ourselves?" You'll see that this type of question is likely to stop both you and others in your tracks, preventing you from staying in Problems and Drama. It's really that simple, yet incredibly powerful.

After reviewing the Five Levels, my client, Robert, realized that he and his peers had indeed been stuck in Drama and Problems. They were thinking in terms of "me vs. you" or "us vs. them." He knew that if he helped himself and everyone else move into a common vision (where the organization wanted to be), it would shift everyone's mindset to a higher level of "we." That's why the Vision and Planning levels are where the best self-leaders focus.

Robert ended up bringing in an outside facilitator for an off-site training session, and the group of division heads spent the day creating an agreed-to joint vision—reflecting the "we" perspective. The group then looked at what they and their respective teams were doing well (and not so well) that would promote or hinder that vision. It soon became clear that their current inability to work together effectively would keep all of them—and the organization as a whole—from succeeding unless they did something collectively to fix it.

That powwow launched a two-year initiative to break down the company's "concrete silos." Ultimately, the organization became even more successful than they had envisioned that day, exceeding their goals and achieving steady growth that stretched beyond their expectations. Perhaps even more importantly, the culture of the organization has changed from divisiveness and in-fighting to a place where smart professionals *want* to work, boosting the organization's retention efforts in a very competitive talent market.

All of it started when Robert took the initiative to recognize a challenge. This just shows that when we work on our own self-leadership skills, we also set an example that can have a significant and positive ripple effect on others.

I often suggest my clients create a Five Levels of Focus reminder and post it on their wall or near their computer screen—someplace where they will see it regularly. It then becomes a regular habit to ask yourself, "At which level am I focusing right now?"

The Self-Leader as Mediator and Peacemaker

At some point, you will likely encounter conflict between others in the workplace, no matter how much you try to prevent it. Here are some tips clients have implemented to mediate disagreements when they arise. Remember: No two conflicts are exactly the same, so it's important to figure out the best way to deal with each specific situation.

- **Don't ignore conflict, expecting it to take care of itself.** If you choose to hide your head in the sand when tensions arise, conflicts will likely grow and get worse, even spiraling out of control. Great self-leaders address conflict from the moment it first appears.

- **Be careful not to take sides.** Respect should be shown to everyone you work with, even if you are absolutely sure someone is wrong. Publicly chastising that individual reflects poor self-leadership on your part.

- **Separate facts from assumptions and beliefs.** Sometimes, a dispute can be resolved quickly if the parties discover that their assumptions and beliefs are false. If individuals differ on what they see as "facts," gather evidence to find out what really happened. As much as possible, don't focus on the past, but stay focused on moving forward. Ask each person involved what they would consider to be the ideal outcome of this conflict and how they would suggest the situation be resolved.

- **Review the Five Levels of Focus with the people involved.** Ask them how they could get out of Problems and Drama and focus on Vision and Planning. Ask them also to be careful how they handle focusing on Details. Sometimes, people use details to inadvertently create conflict, diving into the "nitty gritty" when it won't really move the conversation forward.

- **Agree to disagree.** Encourage everyone to treat each other with respect and move forward toward the stated vision. If you're a good self-leader, you'll be able to step back once those who were arguing are on the right track, and let them find their own way toward shared goals.

The next time you find yourself facing a conflict and unsure about what to do, try the "What You Think Is What You Get" Triangle, or assess where you and the others involved stand in terms of the Five Levels of Focus. Chances are, these two simple but powerful tools will allow you to self-lead through the conflict with finesse.

9

Limiting Self-Leadership Behavior #8:

Not Being Ready for the Challenges of Today's Diverse Workplace

Today's workplace is the most diverse in the history of humankind. Just how diverse? Pause for a moment, and think about it. You may not believe you deal with that many different types of people on a regular basis. But even if you aren't in an international corporation working across multiple countries, you still probably have people around you who are of various generations, marital statuses, religions, and sexual orientations. I suspect diversity is more prevalent in your life than you think.

Besides the people within your work world, what about the people you talk to on the phone and meet within your community? When you call a customer service number, for example, you might speak to someone in another country. Stop and try to count how many different nationalities you encounter during a typical month. The *minimum* that members of my audiences usually average is around five. Many of them have much higher numbers, upwards of 10-15.

If people had been asked that question 20 years ago, the answer would have been completely different. Why is that?

When I present to leaders about today's diverse work world, I ask someone from the audience to stand up with their arms outstretched. I stand at the tip of the longest finger on that person's right hand and say, "Let the tip of this fingernail represent the first evidence of human beings on earth." Then, to fast forward through time, I walk over to the tip of the longest finger of that person's *left* hand, and say, "If you shave just a tiny sliver off this fingernail, that represents the amount of time that we've been living in the *industrial revolution*, with access to electricity and mass production."

Then, I continue by saying, "Now, if you take no more than *one atom* from the sliver of that fingernail, that represents how long we've been experiencing the level of diversity found in today's workplace." So, what we are facing in today's work world is an *unprecedented experiment*—an ongoing learning lab—and there is no textbook for it. We're all just trying to figure it out as we go along. That's yet another reason why self-leadership is so critical, now more than ever: We are all learning how to maneuver our way through our current, more-complex-than-ever organizations.

Why have our workplaces become so much more diverse? Several reasons:

- The technological revolution, which has brought better international communications, means that companies and organizations can now operate more easily on a 24/7 basis all around the globe.

- International financial and banking integration has reduced barriers to the movement of capital.

- Global trading blocs (the EU, ASEAN, NAFTA, etc.) have reduced national trade barriers.

- Pressure on companies to expand beyond national borders has driven multinational corporations into more emerging geographies and economies.
- Increased gains have come from exploiting economies of scale, which includes outsourcing specific work to countries across the globe.
- Lower international transportation costs have made moving goods from one country to another more cost-efficient.

All of this has also increased the mobility of labor. People are more willing to move to far-flung locations in search of work, and the idea of traveling to another country for a job is not as far-fetched as it was in the past. My own personal case in point: Earlier in my career, when I planned to move from the United States to Poland for my job, my family and friends reacted with horror. They thought I was absolutely insane! "Why would you ever do that?" they asked. Contrast that with today: Consulting firm BCG recently conducted a survey with more than 200,000 participants from across the globe which showed that, on average, almost 64% said they would be willing to move to another country for work.[6]

This heightened mobility means that, for an ever-increasing number of people today, the language they grew up speaking is not the primary language they use at work. If this applies to you, too, you know what a challenge that can be. If this isn't your experience, just reflect for a moment about what it would be like to consistently use another language on the job. This is just one more challenge of the modern-day workplace.

All of this unprecedented diversity in the work world has multiple benefits for both employees and companies alike. But it also has a potential downside: It increases the potential for at-work conflict.

---

6. Strack, Rainer; von der Linden, Carsten; Booker, Mike; Strohmayr, Andrea, "Decoding Global Talent—Workers' Increasing Mobility," *BCG Perspectives.com*, https://www.bcgperspectives.com/content/articles/human_resources_leadership_decoding_global_talent/?chapter=2.

Unconscious Bias

What is at the heart of the conflicts found in today's increasingly global and diverse workplace? Unconscious bias. Many of my clients deny that they have any bias at all. Perhaps you're thinking the same thing right now: "I'm not biased!" Some individuals might even have a knee-jerk negative reaction to that word. "No way! I promise you, Brenda," people have said to me, "I am definitely *not* biased."

But the truth is that we *all* have some form of unconscious bias. Remember that it's *unconscious,* so we're not even aware of it unless we make the effort to be.

What is "unconscious bias," exactly? Here's the definition I like to use:

> *Our implicit people preferences, formed by our socialization, our experiences, and our exposures to others' views about various groups of people.*

Our bias occurs in the quick, unconscious judgments we make about others. Indeed, research shows that our brains are programmed to subconsciously and immediately notice four things about somebody when we first meet them:

- Gender
- Age
- Ethnicity
- Physical attributes such as height, weight, or a disability

How do we know that? In real-world "change-blindness" research, volunteer participants entered an office one at a time, where a white male in a suit and tie stood behind a reception counter and welcomed them. He asked each person to sign a form, and while they did, he said, "I'll get your badge for you." As he ducked down behind the reception counter, another white male—who wore a similar-looking suit—emerged from behind the counter and handed over the badge.

Each research participant was then taken into another room where they were interviewed. "How many individuals did you interact with in the reception area?" they were asked. The response was typically "One." Most of those interviewed didn't even believe it when they were told that they had actually interacted with two different people. They had to be shown a video of the encounter as proof.

The experiment was repeated, and this time, the second man to emerge from behind the reception desk was wearing a shirt and tie but no jacket. Again, no one noticed the differences between the two men. This experiment was conducted again and again, and the only time when the majority of the participants noticed that they were interacting with a different person than the original greeter was when the person who stood up behind the counter was someone of a different gender, age group, or skin color.

Dr. Binna Kandola OBE and Dr. Nic Sale of Pearn Kandola have conducted extensive research to demonstrate the pervasiveness of unconscious bias. They contend that our physical brains haven't changed in tens of thousands of years … but our environment certainly has! Despite modern-day changes, we still respond to our world the same way cavemen did millennia ago in terms of our innate fight-or-flight response. As such, we are programmed to make instant conclusions about people in order to ensure our safety.

Without realizing it, whenever we meet someone new in our day-to-day lives, we subconsciously and consistently ask ourselves, "Am I safe with this person? Do I need to fight with him/her, or should I flee for my life?" The outcome of that causes us to "file" people into categories in our mind so that we can try to predict how they will behave. We are much more comfortable once we can label someone as belonging to a particular category.

We base these categories on what we've been taught. Many of the assumptions we make were planted in our brains when we were very young. Remember, these assumptions and beliefs exist beneath the surface of our conscious minds! So, when we experience one person with certain attributes, we will likely assume that the next person with similar attributes will behave the same way. When we do this, we fail to take *individuality* into account, and this is how stereotypes are created.

But in today's inclusive and diverse world, stereotypes are not only unreliable, they are flat-out incorrect.

Taking This to the Streets

Just how much and how automatically do we categorize people? We decided to take this experiment to the streets. We armed ourselves with photos of three different people—a Caucasian woman, an Asian woman, and an Indian man. Each looked disheveled, wore clothes that weren't very nice, and frowned/had an unsettled look on their faces. We then intercepted people on the streets and asked them to give us their first impressions of those individuals.

To avoid any racial bias, we only asked Caucasians about the Caucasian woman, only asked Asians about the Asian woman, and only asked Indians about the Indian man.

Every single interview revealed the same responses: People immediately described these individuals as "down on their luck," not working, divorced, of low socio-economic status. Comments like, "He's not married," or "She's very unhappy at work" were commonplace.

Then, we took photos of the same three people, but this time, we dressed them in nice business clothes. They wore glasses, and their faces were either smiling and/or looking more confident.

We showed these new photos to the same people on the street. First of all, they didn't recognize that the actors were the same as in the first images. This time, though, they described the three individuals as "successful," "married with two or three children," "in a good job," "good at time management," etc.

What was most fascinating about the experiment was not that people have different impressions—after all, we all know that first impressions count—but it was the extent to which the people interviewed made up *detailed stories* about the strangers in the photos. It was a tangible example of the brain's hard-wired, fight-or-flight response at work. The faster we can judge and make assessments about someone, the faster our brains can file them into a category of "friend or foe."

We do this all the time at work. When we see a secretary wearing flip-flops, or a young man with a pilled shirt collar, or someone carrying lunch to work in an unsightly plastic grocery bag, we come up with all sorts of unconscious bias descriptors—lazy, clueless, messy, poor, no friends, can't hold a job, loser. Think about it for a moment: When has someone made a snap judgment about you that had nothing to do with the truth? We've all experienced it, yet we continue to do it—unconsciously—to others.

As the experiment showed, unconscious bias can also lead us to *positive* conclusions about a person that may or may not be true: A woman wearing a tailored suit and carrying a designer handbag triggers a bias of success. We may think she manages her money well, had a good upbringing, and is self-confident. A man wearing a cashmere sweater and driving a Mercedes evokes the same impression, though in reality, he might have been born into money and may never have worked a day in his life. Or he could be a drug dealer. Who knows? But it just goes to show that our assumptions are instinctual, happening lightning-fast in our programmed brains.

Research indicates that unconscious bias exists in everyone in the workplace, and it can have a significant impact on our successes and failures, particularly when it comes to good self-leadership. Considering today's diversity, can you see how unconscious bias can be very dangerous? We can no longer afford to judge people based on first impressions. Given the thousands of variables that shape our lives and behaviors today, there are fewer extremes now. Indeed, today, almost *everything* happens "in the gray."

Yet, the stereotypes that we have created in our brains are tenacious. We humans hate to leave our comfort zones, so once we have a bias, it can be extremely difficult to change. While the fight-or-flight response has good intentions—we are hard-wired to protect ourselves—we need to update our brains for the 21st century. Think of it as moving from Brain 1.0 to Brain 2.0!

Three Steps to Diminishing Bias

It takes good self-leadership and constant vigilance to diminish bias, but I have found three key steps that we can all take to do just that:

1. Acceptance
2. Awareness
3. Action

Let's look at all three.

1. *Acceptance.* As a first step, we must recognize and admit that bias exists and that, as individuals, we are all biased in some way or another.

Our brains often make "cognitive shortcuts" for us, but those shortcuts aren't particularly accurate because we don't really think things through. Our brains skip thoughtful processes and go straight to the conclusions they want to make without gathering any meaningful information about the individuals involved.

To illustrate this, take a look at the drawing on the next page. Without overthinking it, what is the first thing you see?

Did you see a duck … or a rabbit?[7] If you look closely, you can see both, depending on what your brain tells you. This exercise illustrates just how quickly our brains try to make sense of what we see, even if it isn't exactly the truth.

---

7. No one seems to know the origins of this drawing, but it first appeared in the 23 October 1892 issue of *Fliegende Blätter*, a German humor magazine.

Why do we do this, and why is it so hard to change our minds? Because *we want to be right*. Research indicates that it actually feels good to be right because when you are, the brain releases a feel-good chemical called dopamine. On the other hand, it *feels bad to be wrong*. In fact, when you are wrong, your brain actually triggers the same type of emotional pain that you would feel if someone stepped on your toe.

You can see now why there is such resistance to seeing ourselves as biased. It's literally "painful" to think of ourselves as wrong. Case in point: Even after I've illustrated clearly to audiences that we are all biased, when I ask them to answer "agree" or "disagree" to the statement "I am biased," up to 20% may still answer "false." (By the way, that is what is called "Blind Spot Bias," which is the belief that everybody else is biased, but not you.)

Entire *systems* can be biased, too. A study conducted several years ago of students at a leading U.S. business school showed that women and international students were failing at a much higher rate than American men. Grading for each course was based 50% on class participation and 50% on reading, analyzing, and writing recommendations for real-life case studies.

The professors at the time were almost all men. During class discussions, it was not unusual for male students to make comments like, "I totally disagree with what you just said, and I'll tell you why!" Research revealed that the male professors would subconsciously see that as demonstrating good, solid communication. When a woman raised her hand, however, she might respond with something like, "I understand why you might think that way, but actually, I see it differently. Let me explain." Results of the study showed that response was generally perceived as "weak" by male professors, so women received poorer grades for class participation.

Meanwhile, it was also uncovered that international students at the school were having trouble with the case study analysis required to earn a passing grade. Native-English students could read the case studies and write an analysis within the allotted four-hour exam period. However, due to a deficit in their English reading and writing comprehension, non-English speakers would spend the entire exam period just reading the case study material, rarely leaving enough time to get to the analysis and write up their solution for the case. This caused international students to fail at a higher rate.

The outcomes of the research were clear: There were biases inherent in the grading system. As a result, the school quickly took the initiative to hire more female professors and helped bring style bias to the forefront of male professors' awareness. The school also required that all new international students have a much higher-level command of the English language before enrolling.

You can see why accepting that bias exists in us, in others, and even in our systems is the first critically important step to diminishing bias in the workplace.

2. *Awareness.* The next step is to *become aware of your biases* and the various types that exist. If you pay attention to bias while it's happening, you can interrupt it before it causes problems. This involves labeling the bias so that, whenever you form an opinion about someone or something, you can ask yourself, "What is the lens through which I am viewing this?"

Over 150 different types of bias have been identified, but for our purposes, I'll outline the six most common types I regularly see in the workplace.

- **Similar-to-Me Bias.** Answer honestly either true or false to this statement: "In a professional social setting (formal networking event, going out for lunch, drinks after work, etc.), I tend to want to spend time with colleagues who are most like me."

    If you're like the majority of people who attend my programs, you answered "True." In fact, on average, 85-100% of attendees answer "True" to this question.

    What's wrong with wanting to spend time with people who are like us? Here are a couple of examples of what happens as a result of Similar-to-Me bias in the work world:

    ➢ The division leadership team of a large Asia-based multi-national corporation unknowingly and consistently recruited and hired people who were *just like themselves*. When I applied a behavioral assessment to the team, we discovered that all of the top layers of leadership had almost identical behavioral styles. So, as they recruited new employees, the team became "lopsided" without the other kinds of skills it needed to function well as a whole. If they had hired people who were different from themselves, they would have had a better-rounded team and could have benefited as an organization from a variety of thinking styles and behaviors.

    ➢ For an upcoming promotion, an executive was faced with choosing between two direct reports, Jenna and May. The exec got along well with Jenna because both the executive and Jenna were outgoing, married, and bonded over stories about their kids. But Jenna had some clear behavior deficits: She didn't consistently meet deadlines, and the quality of her work wasn't always up to par. Meanwhile, May was shy, single, and didn't socialize much beyond work hours. But she always met her deadlines and produced good work. The executive chose to promote Jenna. Why? Similar-to-Me Bias had kicked in.

- **Confirmation Bias.** When we have this bias, we look for and find evidence that confirms our beliefs, while ignoring evidence that doesn't support those beliefs. How does this work? Let's say you have a new team member who turns in his first document to you for review. It's terrible—poorly written, not structured, and strategically off. It's highly likely that, from that moment on, every time this employee turns in a document, you'll anticipate lousy work. Even if he improves, you will most likely attribute the improvement to something else. "He must have gotten help," you might think. Confirmation bias has us wanting to be right even if it means ignoring facts.

  Here's an example of confirmation bias in recruiting: A study showed that in a 30-minute job interview, the interviewer spends the first four minutes coming up with a hypothesis: *Is this person right for the job or not?* The next 26 minutes is spent trying to confirm the hypothesis. That's an example of just how much we want to "prove" we're right.

- **In-Group/Out-Group Bias.** If you have this bias, you perceive people who are similar to you more positively than people who are different from you. We feel better about ourselves when we're with a group of people who are like us. They become our "in-group," while others who are different become members of our "out group."

  Professor Kandola explained the implications of this bias when it comes to performance appraisals: We trust the people in our in-group more, so we put them under less scrutiny and think more positively about what they do. At the same time, we tend to focus on the negatives of the out-group members, so we put them under more scrutiny. Ultimately, there is more favorable bias toward the in-group members, who may get better performance appraisal outcomes but with less evidence. If both groups were under *equal* scrutiny, however, we might actually find that the in-group's performance scores would go down.

  Here's an example of this bias in action: The executive in charge of a team wanted to build camaraderie, so he encouraged everyone on the team to get together for lunch twice a week. During those lunches, the group focused mostly on the personal side of life.

Given that most of the team members were big sports fans, the conversation tended to drift in that direction.

There was one female team member, and she wasn't into sports. As a result, she mostly felt left out of those conversations, awkward, and not able to contribute. Her attempts to change the subject were largely ignored; the group would quickly move right back onto the topic of sports. Soon, the female team member stopped attending the lunches and eventually asked for a transfer to a different team. Due to in-group/out-group bias, the team leader's attempts to build camaraderie not only backfired, but caused him to lose a good employee.

- **Halo Effect Bias.** When you let someone's positive qualities in one area influence your perception of him/her in other areas, you are experiencing Halo Effect Bias. For example, there's a tendency to believe tall people make good leaders. Height has nothing to do with leadership ability, of course, but we subconsciously perceive that it does. Most U.S. presidents have been above average in height, for example.

  How does this play out in the workplace? A sales professional may be good at bringing in new accounts and generating revenue, so she gets promoted to a higher-level position, such as Vice President of Sales. Unfortunately, that individual may not know the first thing about being a company executive. This happens at alarming frequency in many companies.

- **Curse of Knowledge Bias.** In this case, the more you know, the harder it is to appreciate the perspective of those who know less. This can have powerful implications in today's workplace—older staff may see younger workers as lacking basic skills, while millennials might perceive older workers as incompetent with technology. It can also cause you to have a bias against international employees, whom you may perceive as knowing less about your culture, especially if they are not 100% fluent in the language used at work.

- **Fundamental Attribution Error Bias.** When you have this bias, you believe that your own errors or failures are justifiable due to *external* circumstances, but others' errors or failures are due to *internal* factors. For example, if you get fired, you might blame it on a poor economy. But if a colleague is fired, you might say, "He got fired because the quality of his work isn't that good." Once again, this demonstrates just how strongly we try to avoid the possibility of being wrong.

What Biases Have YOU™ Seen in Your Workplace?

Not surprisingly, when I ask executives which of these six biases they have experienced or witnessed in their organizations, most respond, "All of them!"

How about you? Review the biases in the chart, and make note of which ones you've experienced in your workplace, either in yourself or in others.

Type of Bias	Definition	Have you seen/experienced this bias in your workplace?
Similar-to-Me Bias	The tendency to like people who are like you	Yes____ No____
Confirmation Bias	Looking for and finding evidence that confirms your beliefs, and ignoring evidence that does not support those beliefs	Yes____ No____
In-Group/Out-Group Bias	Perceiving people who are similar to you more positively than people who are different from you	Yes____ No____
Halo Effect Bias	Letting someone's positive qualities in one area influence your perception of him/her in other areas	Yes____ No____
Curse of Knowledge Bias	The more you know, the harder it is to appreciate the perspective of those who know less	Yes____ No____
Fundamental Attribution Error Bias	Believing that your own errors or failures are justifiable due to external circumstances, but others' errors are due to internal factors	Yes____ No____

By now, here's what we know about bias:

- It exists in everybody, in the workplace, and even in systems.
- It's impossible to get rid of bias because it's a key part of our hard-wired human nature.
- It can also be difficult to change because, by its very nature, it is unconscious.

Based on this list, it would be easy to perceive bias as insurmountable, and bury your head in the sand! But, there are big benefits to diminishing bias, particularly in the workplace. Since bias can significantly impact both your successes and failures, let's look at what you *can* do to begin to lessen the effects of unconscious bias on the job.

3. Action. The third step to diminishing bias is to *take action*. While no single person can change the entire workplace culture, leaders can do a lot to set the tone for improvement around biases that exist within their organization.

Here are a few great self-leadership tips to help you mitigate unconscious bias:

- When speaking of matters that are potentially related to bias, only use facts, focusing on what you honestly *know* to be true.
- Challenge yourself to see the information from an outside, impartial observer's perspective. If you need help, ask others for their objective perspectives to help you see the situation with fresh eyes.
- Stay alert to your own behavior. Whenever you make a decision that impacts someone else, review the various biases to see if you might be stuck in one or more of them. Be honest with yourself! If you catch yourself jumping to a conclusion or making up your mind before you've heard someone else's opinion or examined the facts, remind yourself of the downsides to this approach and how you would feel if someone did that to you.

- Imagine that you are making the same decision for someone else. How would you see it differently?

- Fast-forward in your mind to how the decision you are about to make will play out in six months' time. This "future-view" can help remove emotions from the situation and make your decision more objective.

- Take a break, and revisit the situation later when you feel fresher and more capable of being objective.

- Use empathy, putting yourself in the other person's/peoples' shoes, and imagine what it feels like to be them. How would they see this differently?

- Focus on the big picture. You and the other individuals involved have shared goals and values somewhere. Focus on those similarities rather than on the differences.

Lastly, and most importantly, speak up when you see bias happening to others. Remember: It's *un*conscious bias, so those around us (including ourselves) are not usually aware that we've jumped to an unfair conclusion about someone, let alone what the impact of that conclusion might be. Keep this gentle challenge handy for when you feel you're experiencing or witnessing bias at work:

"To what extent is bias impacting this decision?"

Perhaps you've not spent much time thinking about unconscious bias before. If you keep a watch-out for it, you'll no doubt find yourself noticing it more and more—in yourself and others—now that you've become aware of it. The more you're able to eliminate it at work, the fairer you'll be with everyone you encounter, and the more harmonious your team, division, and organization will become. It's what great self-leaders do.

10

Limiting Self-Leadership Behavior #9:

Managing Down More Than Up and Across

My client, Ethan, came to me one day, confused and distressed due to the results of his 360-degree feedback report.

The good news was that his direct reports adored him. "Best boss ever!" one had written. Another gushed, "I love coming to work because I get to work for him!" They described him as open-minded, friendly, sincere, a good listener, firm when he needs to be, a boss who clearly communicates his objectives, and then follows up effectively. Clearly, Ethan was doing things right when it came to leading his team.

The not-so-good news came from two other sources—first, from Ethan's two bosses, one direct and one dotted line. These two superiors saw him in a completely different way, evidenced by their critical comments. Here are just a few examples:

- Lacks initiative
- Lacks visibility
- Doesn't facilitate discussions
- Doesn't offer visionary ideas or examples
- Needs to be more tenacious
- Doesn't lead from the front
- Needs to develop a broader network among his peers and next-level managers

The second source of not-so-good feedback came from Ethan's *peers* who were equally critical:

- Should get involved more
- Needs to hold discussions to resolve matters
- Doesn't engage the broader group
- Has unclear objectives
- Communicates poorly
- Doesn't get enough support to make things happen
- Shows a lack of ownership

Ethan was shocked and upset with the results. "How can the outcomes amongst the three groups be so different?"

I asked Ethan to reflect on how much time he spent—in any given week—with direct reports vs. his boss and/or peers. He paused for a second, and then responded, "Come to think of it, I probably spend about 95% of my time with my direct reports."

The "penny dropped," as they say, and Ethan realized he was spending much less time managing "up and across," which automatically meant that his bosses and his peers simply didn't see him in action all that much. The feedback was a clear indication that Ethan wasn't giving all of his stakeholders the same amount of attention.

It also indicated what Ethan confirmed: that dealing with direct reports was his comfort zone. He admitted that he was much less comfortable interacting with peers and bosses. As such, he was subconsciously avoiding those two groups as much as possible, causing a steady deterioration of his relationships with them. Ethan had always just assumed that if he and his team performed well and delivered (as had been the case in all of his past positions), he would be fine.

I have seen this challenge with multiple coaching clients. When you are at the mid-level of an organization, you are learning how to get results from the individuals and teams you supervise. So, it's understandable that you would focus on "managing down." After all, early in your career, leading staff is a major factor in your success; it helps you get promotions, raises, and gain status and a positive reputation within the organization.

But that isn't how it works as you move up to higher positions. With increasing necessity, balancing time with *all* stakeholders becomes more critical. Indeed, managing "up" to superiors and "across" to same-level colleagues becomes just as important as managing down. Let's explore this common gap in a senior leader's self-leadership arsenal.

Don't Forget to Accentuate the Positive

A Regional CEO client of mine, Ahmed, had two bosses—both global CEOs and both in different, far-flung countries, several time zones away from where Ahmed was located. Knowing that both bosses were extremely busy, Ahmed was always reluctant to "bother them," so he didn't interact with them very often. When he did reach out, it was usually to get advice on a substantial difficulty—one that, in his mind, was major enough to justify calling a high-level leader.

Ahmed thought he was being smart and considerate by only disturbing these two busy and important leaders when he needed them. At first glance, that seems very respectful of him, right? Well … not so much. In fact, in verbal feedback, Ahmed's two bosses both revealed that they saw him as "the leader who only has problems and can't seem to resolve them himself."

Ahmed was making a critical error that I often see in my coaching clients: He wasn't doing anything to showcase the decisions that were going *well* for him and his division. He didn't showcase when operations were running smoothly. He didn't share when he and his team experienced positive outcomes. Instead, he was only reaching out and sharing "up" the key issues and major problems he was facing.

The moral of the story? It's critical to maintain a healthy ratio of positive-to-negative communication with your boss. And by "healthy ratio," I mean for every one problem you send his or her way, share at least *five* positives—either for you, your team, or both.

In fact, I contend that it's actually your *job* to keep bosses informed of the good things happening in your area—not just for your own career success, but so that senior leaders can use your information to make informed decisions affecting their area of the organization. This is an incredibly important aspect of managing up, and one that is often overlooked. (It's so important that we will also discuss it in more detail in the chapter on self-promotion and visibility.)

When it comes to managing "up," here's another error I often see: focusing more on the "direct" boss than the "dotted line" boss. It's easy to make this mistake since it will most likely be the direct boss who will write your year-end performance review and be in charge of finalizing your raises and bonuses. But don't forget that, in today's heavily matrixed world—where it's not unusual for one leader to have multiple dotted line bosses inside the organization—input from those dotted line bosses can have a powerful impact.

So, it's important to find a balance between your two (or more!) bosses in today's increasingly complex reporting-line structure and to make sure that all important members of top management know what's happening in your part of the organization.

Don't Just Coach "Down"—Coach Up and Across, Too

When a new boss took over her division, my client, Marilyn, found out just how difficult it can be to manage up. Her previous superior had been a very hands-off leader, trusting the individuals who reported to him to know their jobs and to perform them well. But the new boss was a micromanager; he insisted on checking all of his direct reports' work and making them explain and justify every decision. This new style was a big shift for Marilyn, and because she wasn't accustomed to working under anyone's thumb, the relationship with her new boss got off to a rocky start.

Knowing that she needed to make this relationship work, Marilyn approached me for coaching. Based on our discussions, she began proactively engaging her boss more and more, making it a habit to "communicate up" more frequently so that the new boss would always know what she was doing—*before* he asked. She put herself in his shoes, realizing that was what he needed (since he was new to the organization), and made a conscious effort to keep him abreast of all that she was planning and doing. The results were relatively quick, and it helped to strengthen their relationship almost immediately. Whenever she was about to make a decision or act on something, she reminded herself: Communicate, communicate, communicate!

But after a while, another pattern began to emerge from the boss that rubbed Marilyn the wrong way: He would pose a challenge to which Marilyn would instinctively know the answer, but the boss would insist that she fully explore options A, B, C, D, and E before they could settle on a final solution. That would lead Marilyn and her team to spend time and resources exploring all of those various options, only to come back, present all of their findings, and have the boss agree that Marilyn's original, instinctive answer was indeed the best one.

This happened again and again. The inability of Marilyn's boss to stop sending her and her team on wild goose chases might have been one of *his* self-leadership challenges, but it was also a self-leadership challenge for Marilyn. She kept giving in to his directives, even though it made no sense and wasted precious organizational resources. "I just don't understand how to make this stop!" she confided in me.

So, I asked Marilyn, "If this were an employee of yours exhibiting this behavior, how would you handle it?"

"I would coach the employee. I would ask powerful questions to help him figure out what was causing the behavior."

"Great," I responded. "So, how could you use those same methods in this situation?"

Marilyn looked surprised but intrigued. "I would never have considered holding that same type of coaching conversation with my *boss!* Really?"

How Do You Coach "Up?"

If you're like most leaders, you probably think of "coaching" as what you do when you lead and direct others who work *for* you. But it can also be an extremely effective tool when applied to any relationship, including coaching *up* to bosses and *across* to peers. Here are a few tips to follow:

- One of the best techniques for guiding bosses and peers to new, more effective behaviors is to first, make an objective, factual statement, and then ask powerful, open-ended questions that are aimed toward the big-picture, higher-level arena within the organization. It takes a bit more time and creativity than simply telling bosses and peers what's on your mind, but asking good, strategic, open-ended questions builds relationships, trust, and transparency and can have positive, long-lasting effects.

    By open-ended questions, I mean questions that don't elicit a one-word "yes" or "no" response but require the other person to elaborate. By a*sking* and not *telling,* you will get others to pause, reflect, grow, and come up with answers.

- Pick the right time. Neither you nor your superior or peers should be in a rush or tired at the end of a long day.

- Get into a good frame of mind. Approach the conversation with curiosity. You're here to explore, so don't go into the discussion attached to a specific desired outcome or expectation.

- Get out of the "you vs. me" mindset, and rise up into "we." Ask yourself: What positive outcomes can come from this conversation that will not just help us work together more effectively, but will support the overall objectives of our team, our function, and the organization?
- Prepare—and practice out loud—the words you want to say until it sounds natural and you feel comfortable.

With this in mind, here is a snapshot of what happened when my client, Marilyn, coached "up" to her boss, Dirk.

She started off with, "Dirk, I'd like to talk to you about a trend I'm seeing and get your input. I've noticed that when you've asked me to explore solutions to challenges we're facing, I tend to have a 'gut' reaction as to what the top one or two options are, based on my experience. However, to respect your concerns, we continue to go quite deep into exploring multiple choices, taking time, money, and resources to do so. In the end, we almost always revert back to the one or two options I first envisioned.

If we could get to a place where we wouldn't have to explore so many options—if we could just focus on the top one or two—it would save us time, money, and resources. To what extent are you open to exploring this together?"

Because Marilyn positioned this as a benefit for the entire team, Dirk agreed that it was worth considering.

With Dirk aligned to move forward with the conversation, Marilyn continued, "When you ask us to go deeper and explore multiple options, what are your biggest concerns, and what do you hope to achieve?"

It turns out that Dirk simply didn't yet understand the business as well as he wanted, given that he was still relatively new in the company. So, he was using these challenges as a way to increase his own knowledge of what various options looked like. Given the open conversation and environment Marilyn had initiated, Dirk also confided that he was feeling quite a bit of pressure from *his* boss due to new regulations in the industry. That was adding further fuel to his over-the-top dive into details.

Marilyn responded, "I appreciate you sharing that, and I can imagine the pressure you're under. Even though you and I haven't been working together all that long, please know that I have the best interests of the company at heart. I would never recommend anything that would cause us to be out of compliance or result in any issues for the organization. We're definitely in this together!"

This initiated a promise from Dirk to rely more on Marilyn's initial recommendations while asking her to spend more time answering his "lack-of-knowledge" questions about other options they decided *not* to explore.

The result? Within a reasonably short period, not only was Marilyn's team wasting less time on useless option exploring, but Dirk became less of a micro-manager, and Marilyn and Dirk definitely improved their relationship going forward.

Do you see how coaching up meant that Marilyn didn't have to explain or share her *frustrations* with Dirk? Instead, it was all about staying objective and doing the right thing for her team and the company. This also helped her come across as a strong self-leader—exactly the image she wanted.

Managing Peers: How "Connected" Are YOU™?

Two executives, Joelle and Hritesh, were partners in the same law firm. Their styles and priorities were vastly different: Joelle consistently built her internal network, taking time for peer lunches, connecting with fellow partners for dinners, and setting aside work for five-minute chats with colleagues in the office. She also took time to connect people she knew with each other, helping them build their own networks and relationships. In short, she demonstrated good self-leadership when it came to managing *across*.

Hritesh's focus, however, was primarily external, and he spent the bulk of his time satisfying clients and bringing in business. He didn't really see the importance of building internal relationships—after all, he had cases and files to move off his desk, and there never seemed to be enough hours in the day for anything else.

Both partners brought in roughly the same amount of revenues, and for a while, they were at the same level in the firm's organizational structure. But within just three years, Joelle had advanced very quickly, catapulting herself up not just one, but *two* levels higher within the firm. Hritesh, on the other hand, remained in the same post despite his aspirations to move up. His one key mistake: He hadn't built solid internal relationships.

It isn't uncommon for people to reach levels close to the C-Suite and not make it to the highest echelons of the organization because of one thing: *They didn't cultivate positive relationships with their peers on the way up.* Learning to manage across is a very important self-leadership skill. After all, a peer today may become your boss or your subordinate tomorrow.

Your Tasks vs. Relationships Ratio

It's far too easy to focus on your to-do list while neglecting the need to keep building and strengthening your networks, both internally and externally. Part of self-leadership is managing all facets of your work life, and strong networks are a critical part of that.

To help you gauge how you're doing with managing relationships in your network, refer back to the "strategy vs. execution ratio" you worked on in Chapter 4. This time, you'll use the same "circle exercise" to assess how you are doing when it comes to dividing the time you spend on tasks vs. relationships.

Draw a circle on a plain sheet of paper, and look at your calendar over the course of any given week. What's the portion of a typical week that you devote to completing tasks (doing work), as opposed to the portion you spend grooming relationships with stakeholders, in general? Divide the circle into a pie chart, with one section signifying the total time you spend on tasks and the other signifying the total time you spend on relationships. How do the two compare? Are you devoting enough time to developing good connections?

Now, take some time to identify all of the key stakeholders in your work life—direct boss, dotted line boss(es), peers, subordinates, colleagues (current and former), past bosses, external association members, ex-colleagues who now work in other organizations, and on and on.

Draw another circle that will represent the total time you spend networking. How would you divide up this new pie graph into time spent with *each of the various stakeholders listed*? Are you spending more time with one stakeholder group than others? Are you spending more time networking externally than internally, or vice versa? This is an important perspective to keep in mind and will help you balance your self-leadership energy at the appropriate amounts with the right stakeholders.

The Key to Networking Success: The Big Art of Small Talk

Now that you are clearer on the existing status of your internal and external network, let's address one of the core tenets of networking success: small talk.

Mastering "small talk" can make a big difference in your career. Yet, time and time again, clients tell me they dread it. When I speak to an audience and someone mentions that they hate small talk, I sometimes role-play, acting like I'm an individual who has a lot of trouble with it. I inch my way slowly toward someone in the audience and say, "So … um … hi there … um … how are you?" When they say they're "fine," I say, "Oh good." I look around the room, fumbling for what to say next. "Then … um … do you work in this area?" Once they answer that question, I look stumped. How do I move this conversation forward?

If that sounds a bit like situations you've been thrown into (and suffered through), don't feel badly—you're far from alone! All across the world, leaders tell me they dislike small talk and avoid it at all costs.

But as a self-leader—especially one who's working on expanding and strengthening your network—you will inevitably find yourself in plenty of situations, formal and informal, where you'll have to have small-talk conversations. Improving your skills in this area is vital to self-leadership and to your leadership brand.

Just like asking (and not telling) is a powerful strategy in the workplace, one of the easiest ways to make small talk more comfortable is to ask open-ended questions. Again, if you ask questions that bring only a "yes" or "no" answer or a short one-word response, you've given the other party nothing to latch onto and will likely get nothing back in return—except awkward silence. Questions that start with "What" or "How" will get the other person talking. This is particularly helpful if you are an introvert who hates to talk about yourself. With this strategy, you can just ask a few simple questions and then listen to the other person do the talking.

Examples of open-ended, small-talk questions include: "So, what do you like most about your job?" "How did you get started in the industry?" "How has the business [or organization or industry] changed over the years?"

You could also make statements that encourage the other person to elaborate: "That's interesting … tell me more." Or, "Help me understand what you mean by that." Then, listen with genuine curiosity, remembering that nodding your head and murmuring the occasional "Mm-hmmm" will make sure the other person feels heard.

Keep in mind that good networking is *not about you!* It's about making the other person feel comfortable. The good news is that, as the other person's comfort level increases, your own discomfort level is likely to diminish as well.

Of course, you shouldn't stay completely silent throughout the entire conversation. To find meaningful ways to chime in occasionally, listen carefully for common ground in the other person's responses. Does the individual say anything that you can relate to in your own experience? For example, your conversation partner might say, "I got into the industry because I really love technology; I just can't get enough of the latest breakthroughs." You can respond with, "I'm with you—that's why I got into the industry, too. I have an endless fascination with everything tech." Then, pick up on that commonality and move the conversation forward with, "So, where do you see the next big technology breakthrough coming from?"

Instead of finding yourself in a networking situation with someone you don't know, what if you find yourself at a company event faced with making small talk with a coworker or senior leader? Again, the same guideline applies: Ask open-ended questions rather than tell. If you're talking with someone you don't know well but who's from your workplace, be honest and say, "We've worked together for a while now, and I still don't know that much about you. What do you like to do in your spare time?" Or if it's someone you already know fairly well, you could ask, "How is your son's football team doing this year?"

Here's another powerful suggestion to prepare for your next networking event: The next time you have a small-talk situation coming your way, arm yourself with a list of at least ten possible open-ended questions you can ask that could apply to multiple people and situations. Make sure the questions you have in your arsenal begin with either who, what, when, where, or how (never "yes/no" questions, and avoid "why" questions, too). Examples are: "How often do you attend this type of event?" "Where are you from?" "What is your role at work, and how long have you been holding that position?" "Who is your main contact here, and how do you know them?" "What do you like to do in your free time?"

Of course, don't underestimate the importance of smiling and making eye contact. When the person introduces himself or herself, repeat the individual's first name: "It's nice to meet you, Joseph." Repeating the name makes it more likely you will remember it, and it immediately establishes greater rapport.

Armed with these tips and your top 10 networking questions in mind, you'll be prepared for any event where you need to interact with both strangers and work colleagues. The more you prepare yourself, the more comfortable you'll feel.

Remember: Self-Leadership Moves in All Directions

Excellent self-leaders understand the importance of cultivating relationships with all stakeholder groups and in all directions—up, down, across, as well as inside and outside the organization. How are you doing with your "360-degree" stakeholder management? It's fundamental to building your brand as a leader, both inside your organization and within your industry, too.

11

Limiting Self-Leadership Behavior #10:
Overlooking the Importance of Executive Presence

'm often asked, "What's the most popular topic clients request when it comes to leadership development?"

My answer is "Presence"—specifically Executive Presence. Indeed, I'm frequently asked by corporations to speak at conferences and lead multi-day programs on this very topic. Why? Because Executive Presence is that "special sauce" that separates *good* leaders who "do well" from *outstanding* leaders who are catapulted to the top of their organizations.

Let's face it: Most leaders have good enough technical skills, business acumen, and all-around smarts to achieve a certain level of success in an organization. But a powerful sense of "Presence"—that *je ne sais quoi*—is often what's missing, and that's what prevents many leaders from advancing in their careers.

What is Executive Presence? The way I like to define it is: "a set of attitudes, behaviors, and skills which—when combined—send the right signals, influence others, and ultimately drive results."

If you're a senior leader, you no doubt already have some degree of Executive Presence. It's how you reached your current level in the first place. The most admired people have Executive Presence in abundance—people like Nelson Mandela, Oprah Winfrey, and Richard Branson, to name a few. You know when you've met someone with powerful Presence. You feel drawn to that person and you want to connect with him or her.

"All of that certainly sounds appealing," many clients have told me, "but can Executive Presence really be *developed*?"

"Absolutely," I reply. No one is born with Executive Presence. It is a *learned* self-leadership behavior with multiple facets, and it's strengthened through intention and practice.

There are five activities we do every single day that impact our Executive Presence: our actions, reactions, and the way we look, sound, and think as leaders. So, it's a broad topic and worthy of its own book! But in this chapter, we will focus on three main points: An overview of Executive Presence, a self-assessment of the most critical elements of Executive Presence, and the underlying emotion that drives it all.

Just How Important is Executive Presence?

According to a study of 236 senior executives who make decisions about promotions within their organizations, Executive Presence accounts for more than one quarter of what they look for in someone who is aiming to reach the next level.[8]

---

8. Hewlett, Sylvia Ann; Leader-Chivée, Lauren; Sherbin, Laura; Gordon, Joanne; Dieudonné, Fabiola; "Executive Presence," *TalentinInnovation.org*, http://www.talentinnovation.org/assets/ExecutivePresence-KeyFindings-CTI.pdf.

In another study of the most important traits for Chief Information Officers, thousands of CIOs weighed in. The outcome? Even technology took a backseat to core elements of Executive Presence—Communications and Influence, and Personal and Professional Demeanor. Only Business Knowledge/Acumen surpassed these two leadership characteristics on the list of what's most critical to CIO success.[9]

Many such studies exist, all pointing to one outcome: Executive Presence is fundamental for those who want to reach increasingly higher levels in any organization. And it takes strong self-leadership to stay aware of and demonstrate the specific attitudes, behaviors, and skills required to embody powerful Presence.

The Most Important Ingredient of the "Secret Sauce"

I believe that underlying every aspect of Executive Presence is one core element: confidence—the absolute certainty that you can do what it takes to succeed in any situation. When you have confidence, you believe in yourself, so that—even if you're undertaking something new—you know you'll be able to figure it out when you get there.

Yet, many accomplished leaders lack the confidence they need to cultivate strong Executive Presence. One indication of that: I've met a large number of leaders who suffer from "Impostor Syndrome." That's a term coined in 1978 by two psychologists, Dr. Philine Clance and Dr. Suzanne Imes, which describes high-achieving people who don't really trust their successes. They are constantly afraid of being exposed as a fraud, no matter how much they've accomplished. "I just got lucky," they might say. As much as they want a higher level of responsibility or a specific promotion, deep down they question whether they are good enough to deserve it.

Then, there are other leaders like my client, George, who allowed a setback to damage his confidence. He had 29 years of experience in

---

9. "Gartner Executive Program Survey of More Than 2,000 CIOs Shows Digital Technologies are Top Priorities in 2013," *Gartner.com*, Published January 16, 2013, http://www.gartner.com/newsroom/id/2304615.

the corporate world. For 27 of those years, he was a dynamic go-getter, moving up the ladder and achieving great success every step of the way—not just in his professional life, but in his personal life as well. For the last two years, though, things hadn't gone so well for him.

He had taken over a division that was new to him, and it wasn't performing well under his leadership. He was getting increasing pressure from top management to deliver. In addition, at about that same time, he developed some physical problems, especially joint pain, so he stopped exercising. This left him with far less energy. To make matters worse, George and his wife were divorcing. This combination of events caused George's confidence level to plummet.

When we met, I could sense George's energy. He was like a balloon that had been deflated.

"George, for how many years did you have tremendous success?" I asked him.

"Twenty-seven years," he responded.

"And for how long have things been a bit rocky?"

"These past two years," George replied.

"So, you've had 27 years of positive, ongoing successes, and only two years—24 months—of less-than-positive outcomes. Is that correct?"

I could see the realization of this sinking in. "You're right—I have to keep that in perspective," George said. "I can't let these past 24 months cloud a career and a life that have gone so well. It's only a small portion of the whole."

George is an example of how quickly confidence can fade if you're not careful to nurture it. And once confidence fades, Executive Presence takes a hit.

Keep Your Confidence Level Steady

Perhaps you suffer from Impostor Syndrome, too, or have been dealt a "confidence blow" like George? If so, pause and think about how much you have accomplished. Take an inventory of your successes and how they came about, and you'll most likely recognize that it was definitely *not* "all luck." Your talents, skills, and hard work are why you've achieved success.

Here's an exercise to help you look honestly at what you *have* done and the skills you've developed, while acknowledging what you believe you genuinely lack. Make two columns on a sheet of paper or on your computer, and on the left-side column, list your most valuable attributes. Don't stop adding to the list until you've run out of qualities and skills (and don't be humble!) Then, in the right column, list the areas where you still need work. Be objective about what you could do better. Once done, sit back and review the two lists. If you're like most of my clients, I suspect you'll be surprised at the outcome, because we often underestimate what we *can* do versus what we think we *cannot* do. (George did this exercise, and this one task alone gave him more momentum than he'd had in a long while.)

It's critical to look at yourself the way others do, but it's difficult to see yourself through an objective lens. That's why it's so important to get feedback—and why I've devoted an entire chapter to that topic later on in this book.

The single most powerful and productive exercise I give my clients is the task of keeping a "Confidence Journal." It's simple: As you go through your day, and you have an experience that either increases or decreases your confidence level, write down what happened and why. Whether you are being challenged by a peer, find yourself on the receiving end of a compliment from the CEO, need to fire someone, or are struggling to influence outcomes, make sure to remain objective, and ask yourself: *"What's happening to my confidence right now?"* Go inside and figure out how the experience is impacting you. What's the context? Who's involved, and what's triggering the "boost" or the "bust"? What's *really* causing those ups and downs?

Jot down every incident, and give your confidence level a score based on how you feel: 1 = Not feeling confident at all, 10 = Feeling fully confident. Don't judge yourself as you write—just be objective. Detach emotionally for a moment, and become an impartial reporter of what's happening inside you, noting what triggered your shift in confidence.

Depending upon how many incidences you have, after a week or two of keeping track, pick up your confidence journal, and look for trends. What do you see, objectively? For example, it might be that your confidence level drops when you address very senior leadership, but you feel fully confident when addressing and leading direct reports.

Or maybe you wrote: "When I'm dealing with peers over whom I have no direct authority, my confidence level drops."

Or: "When I'm involved in a conversation in my area of expertise, my confidence is high, but when I'm called upon to discuss areas outside my division, my confidence is reduced."

Some clients keep the journal for two or three weeks, while others like to keep it going for two months or longer. It's up to you. Once you understand the triggers that are causing confidence highs and lows, you'll then be better able to preempt the triggers so that you can avoid confidence dips.

If you strengthen your confidence in this way, you'll be much less likely to allow a setback to diminish your belief in yourself. Keep in mind all of your achievements, and use them to keep you moving forward, even when faced with a challenging situation.

How's Your Executive Presence Doing?

You're now set to better understand your confidence level and keep it from fluctuating, which is a foundational facet of Executive Presence. But what about the many other aspects of Presence?

The following is a self-assessment that highlights what I believe are the 15 most important facets of Executive Presence. This will help you review the current status of your Presence at work.

On a scale of 1 to 10, with 1 the lowest score and 10 the highest, rate yourself in the following Executive Presence attitudes, behaviors, and skills. Be honest!

Facet of Executive Presence	Score
1. I have strong, positive influence on my team, coworkers, colleagues, and superiors.	
2. I manage my emotional reactions well in the workplace, and I stay calm under pressure.	
3. When I need to let someone know I'm unhappy with a situation, I speak to them calmly and assertively. I don't express my feelings in a passive-aggressive way.	
4. I am resilient when pressure builds on the job.	
5. I speak up comfortably in very important meetings and when in the presence of more senior leaders.	
6. When I'm attending a gathering or a meeting, I am able to focus 100% on the topic at hand, without distracting thoughts or checking my phone for messages.	
7. Based on the way others relate to me, I believe I exhibit charisma on the job.	
8. I have inner self-confidence, and I believe in myself.	

Facet of Executive Presence	Score
9. When team members and others push back on my decisions, I manage the situation in a professional, balanced way so that the best choice is made without harming workplace relationships.	
10. I'm capable of thinking on my feet when under pressure.	
11. When I'm called upon to make a presentation, I do so powerfully, engaging my audience from beginning to end.	
12. When conflict arises, I manage it quickly and competently, without damaging professional relationships.	
13. I'm aware of and effectively manage my Executive Leadership Brand, not just within my organization, but also within my industry.	
14. I know how to maneuver office politics with ease.	
15. I use storytelling as a means of engaging others when I communicate.	

Putting Your Self-Assessment to Good Use

Once you've finished your self-assessment, review your scores. If you rated yourself an "8" or higher on all 15 of these Executive Presence attitudes, behaviors, and skills, *well done!* Based on my experience, though, that would be rare. It isn't unusual to discover room for improvement on a fair number of these aspects of Presence.

Reviewing the statements where you scored well, ask yourself what prompted you to give yourself that high rating. How do you manage your self-leadership in such a way that you excel in those situations?

Now, look at the statements that scored lower, and write down two or three aspects of Presence that you would like to improve in the coming weeks and months. Once you've identified those priorities, here are just four of many ways to succeed at enhancing your skills:

1. Find role models (boss, peer, colleague, board member, et al.) who you feel embody that particular aspect of Presence, and connect with them to find out how they have managed to succeed in that area. Let them know you're trying to upgrade your own skill and that you want to get their perspective on how you can make it happen. You might even ask if you can observe them in action and take note of what they do to excel in that specific characteristic of Executive Presence. Make a plan for what you can do to emulate those individuals. What action will you take? By when? What does success look like? Be specific.

2. Enlist an "accountability buddy" to support you in developing your Presence, and share your step-by-step plan with him or her. Ask your buddy to follow up with you at regularly scheduled times and to give you honest feedback as you progress.

3. To help you see the challenge from an objective perspective, enlist an expert such as an executive coach or an internal mentor.

4. Attend a course in Executive Presence. If there's a graduate business school in your city, check to see if such a course is offered. Or consider becoming a member of an association that builds expertise in the area in which you want to improve. For example, if your most frequent lack of confidence (translate: jitters!) occurs before you have to give a presentation or speech, you might look up your local chapter of Toastmasters International, a group that has helped millions conquer their fear of public speaking.

The effort it takes to create Executive Presence carries a big return on investment, paying itself back many times over. So, focus on cultivating your self-confidence, and work on the various aspects that make up Presence. It's one of the most powerful self-leadership skills there is, and it's also one of the fastest ways to build the career trajectory you want.

12

Limiting Self-Leadership Behavior #11:
Underestimating the Significance of Self-Promotion and Visibility

I once worked with a leader named Margaret, a Human Resources executive who, along with her team, was responsible for 125 leaders within her large organization—no small feat. However, as a result of a company merger, Margaret and her team suddenly found themselves responsible for almost double that—245 leaders—and were informed that, due to cost-cutting measures, they would have no additional staffing. So, overnight, Margaret and her team were faced with almost double the work and no added help.

Margaret came to me feeling anxious, wondering, "Can we do it? Is it possible?"

She and her team created a vision, devised a strategic plan, worked weekends and late nights, and ultimately did an exemplary job of managing their larger mandate. In fact, within one year, they were working like a well-oiled machine, effectively managing all of the 245 leaders without incident.

When Margaret's annual performance review came, her boss praised her wholeheartedly. He congratulated her on a job well done and let her know just how much the company appreciated what she was able to accomplish.

How did Margaret respond? She shook her head modestly, and said, "Oh, it's OK. It was nothing...."

When Margaret met with me and shared the outcome of her performance appraisal, she must have seen an expression of surprise on my face, given the tremendous effort she and her team had put in during the last year.

She shook her head. "I know, I know. I can't believe I said that!"

After debriefing the situation, Margaret shared that she hadn't taken the compliment well because she was uncomfortable in that moment and didn't want to appear boastful.

Promoting ourselves and talking about our accomplishments in an unboastful way can be uncomfortable for many leaders. It is absolutely true that nobody likes to listen to a braggart going on and on about all the great things he or she has done. But there's a difference between bragging from a place of insecurity that makes you *need* attention, and simply bringing attention to your achievements—with a combination of humility and pride.

Margaret and I talked about how she would have liked to respond to that compliment, and we even prepared a statement that she memorized in case the opportunity arose again. About a month later, Margaret's boss's boss came to see her to also express *his* appreciation for her hard work. This time, she was prepared. When the compliment came, Margaret responded, "Honestly, it took everyone on the team working long hours and even weekends, but I'm really pleased with what we did, and I'm so glad you appreciate it."

By answering in this way, Margaret gave credit to everyone on the team, demonstrating that she is an excellent people leader. But it also allowed for some self-promotion without putting the emphasis only on herself. Then, she brought it back to "*I'm* really pleased with what we did, and *I'm* so glad you appreciate it." As a result, she was able to show awareness of her own accomplishments without resorting to bragging.

Self-Promotion is Self-Leadership

Are you like Margaret? Have you avoided self-promotion out of the fear that you'll be seen as a braggart or as someone who doesn't have humility? I know that being humble is a foundational characteristic in many cultures, and I wholly respect that. But if you avoid promoting yourself on the job, your hard work may go unnoticed. I tell my clients, "Please only learn to be a good self-promoter if you want a successful career and higher compensation!"

Despite the benefits of self-promotion, most senior leaders still avoid sharing their "wins." Some of them think, "It's not that big of a deal. I'll wait until I achieve something bigger, and *then* I'll talk about it."

Others ask me, "Shouldn't talking about my accomplishments be my boss's responsibility?" Well, yes, probably. But let's get real. Put yourself in a modern-day superior's shoes. Financial pressures are creating increasingly flatter organizations, which means bosses have a larger number of direct reports than ever before. Also, the need for companies to go beyond domestic borders to continue their growth trajectory means that not only do bosses have more direct reports, but those direct reports may be located all across the world. So, be empathetic to the fact that top executives' jobs have gotten more and more difficult over the years, and their ability to focus on and promote upwards each individual who works for them has become stretched very thin.

You can now hopefully see how today—more than any other time in the history of modern capitalism—self-promotion has become a vital part of self-leadership. As such, by regularly letting your boss know what you're doing, you are actually making his or her job *easier!* The boss will be grateful because—trust me—when it's time for your yearly performance management review, he/she will be better able to endorse you to upper management. You will not only be helping your superiors, but also demonstrating strong self-leadership and solid Executive Presence in the process.

Another point to consider: By keeping track of your accomplishments along the way, you will be better prepared for your next performance review without the need to invest hours in reflection and writing time. You'll be glad you can avoid that feeling of, "Did I miss anything?" that often accompanies your own self-assessment in annual performance reviews.

How to Self-Promote Without Bragging

Promoting yourself without bragging takes a bit of finesse while you're first learning the art. With that in mind, here are some specific steps you can take:

- Send regular emails to your boss—not about yourself, but about the good work of one or more of your team members. Give those deserving people a spotlight; that will show your superior that you're a terrific leader without taking credit yourself. And, by the way, sending this email about *others'* accomplishments is an excellent way to demonstrate your own *self*-leadership, too.

- Shortly before your performance review, make a list of accomplishments you want to highlight to your boss. This is your chance to let him or her know your strengths. If it helps you feel more comfortable, spend a little time phrasing your remarks so that they don't sound boastful, using proven facts to support your claims. For instance: "The revenues of the Alberta project exceeded expectations by 18 percent, and the strategic plan the team and I put in place reduced costs by 12 percent."

- Don't miss a chance to let someone else praise your good work "upward." If a client, customer, or colleague sends an email expressing gratitude or saying they were impressed with your work or the work of your team, forward it to the boss with a message saying how grateful you are that this person took valuable time out of their day to send positive feedback.

- Always try to applaud another person before you mention your part in a project's success. For example, "Shania worked evenings to finalize this plan, and her efforts really helped me seal this deal. I appreciate having such solid team support." Notice that you use the words "I" and "me" without taking all the credit for yourself.

If you continue to feel uncomfortable when mentioning your own accomplishments, spend time planning the words you will use, as if you were selling a new client on your company's products or services. Practice the phrases at home or with a friend or a peer you trust until you reach a point where sharing your accomplishments feels more natural.

It's Part of Your Job

I mentioned earlier that talking about your achievements makes things easier for your boss. But it's also true that, by not making your accomplishments known, you actually hold back the *organization* from realizing *its* successes, too. Here are a few reasons why:

- Information is power. So, it's likely that sharing your own successful methods could help another individual do his or her job better, too.

- Making others aware of your accomplishments also helps people grasp the "big picture" and to see the puzzle in a more complete way.

- If someone isn't aware of everything that's going on, including what you've achieved, they may not be able to see how *they* can take the organization forward. So, sharing positive outcomes shows everyone in the company how all individuals are interlinked to others. That insight may help them see ways that they, too, can collaborate with colleagues to achieve more.

- When you share with others, it also gives you an opportunity to ask them what they are involved in, and you can then see links and create synergies as well. That will demonstrate to both of you more productive ways of working together.

People who are successful in today's work world no longer think in terms of, "I'm doing this, and you're doing that." Instead, they see it as, "What are we both doing that contributes to the organization?" In other words, when you don't regularly share what you are doing and how it can impact the company as a whole, you're actually being *selfish*. Ever thought of it that way?

Key to success in doing this is not merely "telling" others what you and your team are doing. After sharing what you've done, ask questions like, "How does what I'm talking about relate to what you do, too?" or "What else can I tell you about the work my team and I are doing that might help you in your role?"

Getting Comfortable with Visibility

Increased self-promotion will naturally also increase your visibility within your organization and maybe even within your industry at large. Does the thought of becoming more visible make you nervous? If so, you may be like my client, Carol.

Carol came to me for help in working through her looming visibility problem: She was a senior leader, well-respected in her field, and was about to be tapped for a higher-level position that would give her a lot more visibility across her organization. But she was a natural introvert, so the prospect of having to be constantly "on," with all eyes focused on her wherever she went, seemed exhausting. The new position would be the "crowning glory" of her career, but she was reluctant to accept the promotion for no other reason than she genuinely didn't like the idea of getting non-stop attention.

Carol and I met for a coaching session, and we explored what the concept of "visibility" meant to her. From her perspective, visibility was all about promoting herself, putting herself in the limelight at every opportunity, talking a lot, boasting, and being "out in front" of others.

But those ideas reflect old ways of thinking. In today's world, visibility is viewed not as promoting one individual (Carol), but as promoting and being a representative of your function, your division, the company, and/or your team members, depending on the situation. In other words, Carol shifted her mindset to realize that if she makes her *company* look good, then she looks good, too.

With that new outlook in mind, we considered how all of Carol's various stakeholders might feel if she were to embrace that new line of thinking, shifting the focus away from "her" to "them" (again, meaning the division or company, as the case may be). We came up with these results:

- *Direct Reports:* Carol's increased visibility and focus on others would help direct reports feel more confident and important rather than insignificant—which is how they might feel if she stuck with her old definition of visibility.

- *Superiors:* Those in more senior positions than Carol would feel confident that she was doing a good job and that they had chosen correctly when they appointed her to the higher-level post.

- *Peers:* Colleagues at the same level as Carol would realize she is a team player and that she is taking the bigger-picture/total-company view when representing the organization and when making decisions.

- *Industry Leaders:* Her new view of "visibility" would help external leaders get clear on the message of Carol's company, promoting and building a strong brand for the organization as a whole.

Reviewing this list and envisioning these results gave Carol many more positive feelings about taking on the role. She created a new mantra for herself based on the outcomes—"I'm honored to be able to create visibility *for the company*." That alone helped Carol adjust her feelings about the new post from discomfort and nervousness to reminding herself that it would actually be a *privilege* to support the organization in that way. What happened? Not only was Carol more willing to take on the new, higher-visibility post, but she was actually more excited about it, too.

How Visible Are YOU™, Really?

In my first year of study at Harvard Business School, a large portion of my grade in each course was based on class participation. So, I always had to be aware: Was I speaking up enough? I might talk in one specific professor's class and think that was enough, without realizing that I wasn't speaking up enough in other professors' classes.

To make sure I was participating enough, I started keeping track of how often I spoke in each course and for how long. I was surprised to see that I was doing fine in one course topic, but not in others. This was particularly true if multiple classes (all with different professors) were held in one day. If I had talked quite a bit in one class on any given day, it was easy to overestimate the amount I was contributing in other classes. I clearly needed to put myself "out there" more.

The same dynamic applies to bosses and other superiors. They can only base their impressions of you on the times they've seen and heard you "in action." That's why it's important to project yourself regularly so that superiors and senior leaders have multiple chances to witness you contributing successfully.

Consider these questions, and answer honestly: How often are you creating visibility for yourself by speaking up in management meetings? Are you holding yourself back from contributing? What, exactly, are you offering to move a conversation along? Do you help plot a new strategy, or sit back while others do the real work?

If you aren't sure, I encourage you to start keeping track of your participation in meetings, really getting clear about the value you add.

All you have to do is make a quick mark on a pad during a meeting to make note of how many times you have contributed. Then, after the meeting, consider the *value* that each comment provided. Keep a log of all your meetings with the total number of times you participated. Just disciplining yourself to keep track will bring this to the top of your mind so that you will naturally begin to make sure you're more visible when you are with key people.

Are You Only Raising "Issues" With Your Superiors?

Remember Ahmed from Chapter 10? He didn't want to be seen as "bothering" his bosses, so he only reached out to them at times when he faced a severe challenge. As a result, he became branded as the leader who only had challenges and who never had anything positive to report. That caused his bosses to view him as largely incompetent.

As Ahmed learned, it's important to maintain a healthy ratio of positive-to-negative information that you share with upper level management. For every negative challenge you raise, offset those by sharing five or more positive outcomes you've achieved.

Once Ahmed initiated a twice-weekly update to his bosses, keeping them aware of all of his positives and progress, they did a total about-face where he was concerned: Both bosses were very pleased with his work and pleasantly surprised at his seeming "turnaround." Of course, Ahmed hadn't "turned around" at all! He had just decided to step up and become more visible by regularly sharing more positive outcomes versus only highlighting challenges.

There are good self-promotion lessons in Ahmed's story:

- *Be in touch with your bosses and the senior-most recipients of your work.* Think about how much visibility is necessary for them to be well-informed about what you are achieving.

- *Regularly review and update your list of accomplishments.* Once a month, take time to jot down the successes you've achieved in the past 30 days. This will help you not only prepare for your performance review, but also for those moments when you have a top leader's ear. Make it a habit to reflect: How much are you contributing to the organization overall? What results of your contributions can others actually see? Consistency in doing this review is key! Regularly updating your list will help you make sure your accomplishments are worthy of self-promotion and visibility and will also help you set goals for yourself—another example of good self-leadership.

- *Get specific in your self-review notes—quantify, quantify, quantify.* Those assessing your performance will want to measure your achievements in terms of numbers, so it's important to tangibly quantify the results you're achieving. Thinking of the obvious quantifiable measurements will get you started:

  ➢ Increased sales by ___ percent.

  ➢ Cut costs by ___ percent.

  ➢ Boosted profits by ___ percent.

  ➢ Increased market share by ___ percent.

  Then, quantify results that may be less obvious:

  ➢ Recruited and onboarded ___ new team members.

  ➢ Finished ABC project under budget by ___ percent.

  ➢ Beat deadline for XYZ project by ___ weeks.

  ➢ Increased team engagement scores by ___ percent.

- *Update your CV with this data at least once a year.* Even if you are not currently job hunting—nor have any intention of doing so—schedule a calendar reminder once a year to update your resume. So many executive coaching clients arrive in my office, frantic because they suddenly lost their positions (either through a layoff, a merger, or for other reasons), and their most recent CV is six years old … 10 years old … 14 years old. Don't allow yourself to be that unprepared executive! Strong self-leadership means being prepared and ready for whatever situations might arise.

Here's another reason to keep track of good quantitative outcomes: When clients ask me to review their CVs, I often notice that they haven't included numbers to quantify their successes. Your next senior-level boss will not be motivated to hire you based on phrases like, "Grew the organization through creative solutions," or "Added new acquisitions." Such wording falls dramatically short of showcasing your talents and capabilities.

When you update your CV, you want to see these kinds of notes:

➢ Reversed an underperforming company within 12 months, with revenues up 10% and profits up 24%.

➢ Recruited, trained, and oversaw a 10-member, Director-level team of top global talent, resourced from five different countries.

➢ Boosted Operations' productivity by 31 percent.

➢ Led negotiations and successful completion of a $110-million merger, faster than any in the company's history.

- *Don't let your interview skills get rusty.* Being engaged in self-promotion and visibility means undergoing job interviews from time to time. Why? In senior-level positions, it isn't unusual for companies to use executive recruiters to fill positions.

  A case in point: My client, Renata, was up for a high-level position in the multinational corporation where she had worked for 15 years. Her competition? Two executives from *outside* the company who had been recruited by an external recruiter. So, even if you don't plan to leave your current company, it's a good idea to be prepared for the possibility of an internal job interview, given that you might actually be competing with executives from outside the organization. Think about it: Those external candidates may have a great deal of recent interview experience. Do you?

Renata's situation shows how important it is to regularly practice your interview skills. As such, now and then, when you hear about a position opening up, go through the recruitment/interviewing process. Recruiters will certainly check your LinkedIn profile as part of the process, so don't allow it to stagnate. (Industry colleagues and clients may check your LinkedIn profile as well, so it's always a good idea to keep it up to date.)

Going through the recruitment process now and then will not only help you stay interview-ready but will also help you clarify your value in the marketplace.

One caveat: *Do not* sit for an interview with a direct competitor. That can be viewed as unethical, and you don't want this beneficial exercise to backfire and taint your reputation in the industry. Use your best judgment.

Prepare for Maximum Visibility

Good self-leadership requires getting comfortable with calm, confident, and smart self-promotion, as well as increased levels of visibility. Most executives want to achieve higher and higher positions in an organization, but when that actually happens, it can feel uncomfortable to be so frequently in the spotlight. Nevertheless, it's key to self-leadership success to be prepared for more prominence. Are YOU™ ready?

13

Limiting Self-Leadership Behavior #12:
Struggling with Tough Decisions

As a senior manager or executive, you're constantly faced with difficult decisions. Most of the time, you can make those decisions based on experience, financial analysis of the situation, input from colleagues or your boss, or even perhaps pure instinct. But once in a while—and this happens to us all as leaders—you're faced with a truly gut-wrenching decision that simply has to be made, and there doesn't seem to be any "right" or "obvious" choice anywhere you look.

One of my clients is a perfect example of this. Harry was a senior leader at an international pharmaceutical company. He was usually exhausted, working most of his waking hours. By the time Harry came to me, he was burnt out and ready to give up his career to go live on a beach in Belize. (Well, not literally, but I suspect he could have easily been talked into it …) Through feedback, we uncovered that one of Harry's big issues was decision-making—not in any particular area, but the physical and mental stress of regularly making tough choices. During one of our coaching sessions, Harry and I explored this together.

"What does it feel like when you have to make a decision?" I asked him.

"Painful!" Harry replied.

"Painful," I said slowly. "So, tell me, Harry, how did you decide to marry your wife?"

"That decision? Well, that one was easy," he replied. "I just knew it was the right thing to do."

"So, making *that* decision wasn't painful?" I asked.

"Not at all!" he said, chuckling.

"When you bought the house you live in now, how did you make that decision?"

"Again, that was fairly simple," he said. "My wife and I just walked in, and I just felt it was the right house for us."

"And, again, was that decision painful?" I asked.

"No," Harry replied.

"Got it," I said. "So, it seems not all decisions are painful then—just some. What's the difference between the less painful decisions you've made—the ones we just talked about that seemed so easy for you—and the 'painful' decisions that you mentioned earlier?"

This started an interesting conversation that peeled back the layers around Harry's decision-making process at work. Through the discussion, he revealed that almost everyone he worked with was either a doctor or a scientist—a fairly "left-brained" set of professionals. Based on his experience, those individuals typically felt more comfortable basing their decisions on facts, figures, numbers, charts, and graphs. Harry's colleagues were naturally strong at analytical and linear thinking, and they relied on that for making decisions.

Therefore, for Harry to justify his decisions to his colleagues at work, he had to go through a long and complicated analytical process. This involved explaining to his peers how he had done the analysis, reviewing numbers, and holding lengthy discussions with them that centered on data.

Why was this so exhausting for Harry? Because his natural decision-making style was *intuitive*. If he listened to his gut, he could make decisions quickly because he just *knew* what the right choice would be. But that wasn't happening at work because the professionals he worked with could only be influenced via numbers, facts, and figures. Instead of their guts, his coworkers were using their *heads*.

So, when Harry had to make tough calls, he was subconsciously trying to move into his colleagues' "head space." He attempted to mirror the decision-making process of those he worked with, but that wasn't at all natural for Harry. And that's why he was struggling so much to make decisions—why they were so "painful" for him.

"Great self-awareness, Harry!" I acknowledged. "How will you use this insight to ensure that your decision-making process becomes less painful, quicker, and easier in the future?"

Harry stated that he would first listen to his gut when he had to make a decision, honoring his natural decision-making mode. He would make up his mind based on what his gut told him was the right answer. Then—and only then—would he pull together whatever data he needed to support that initial "gut" decision. Within a few days of implementing this approach, Harry was making decisions faster, easier, and with much less stress. His confidence grew, and the length of his workdays shrunk, leading Harry to feel all-around happier.

An important takeaway from Harry's story is that self-leadership is founded on a solid sense of knowing yourself. What works for you may not work for others, and vice versa.

How do *you* make decisions most comfortably? Whatever your "comfort zone" mode of decision-making, you'll still benefit from learning about other ways that we, as humans, can make choices. Let's explore.

Did You Know You Have Not One, But Three Brains?

That's right—three brains! When most of us hear the word "brain," we think of the organ inside the skull. But Dr. Vikki Brock defines a brain as "a complex and functional neural network that has a memory, intelligence, and control over the decisions we make." With that definition in mind, your body actually comes naturally equipped with three distinct "brains."

1. The first brain, as referred to above, is the one in your **head.** This brain reasons, analyzes, and synthesizes information. You use it for language, telling stories, and thinking things through.

2. The second brain is in your **heart.** Here, you process your emotions, priorities, and values, and it helps you to connect better with others.

3. The third brain is in your **gut.** Here, you find your core identity, the deepest level of "self," according to Brock, so you can use this brain for quick decision-making.

Integration of decision-making through your head, heart, and gut is key to success in self-leadership—trust your gut, listen to your heart, and *then* use your head. Indeed, when all three brains are aligned—when your head and heart and gut agree, and you don't feel conflicted in decision-making—that's when you know you've achieved a high level of self-leadership.

Brock uses a pyramid to illustrate how, in Western, contemporary society, the reliance on the head-brain forms the base of the pyramid; Western leaders tend to use thinking to make decisions rather than the gut.

Western Leadership Model   **Complete-Leader Model**

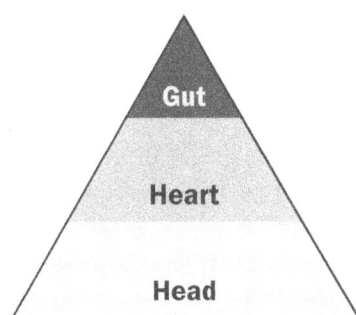 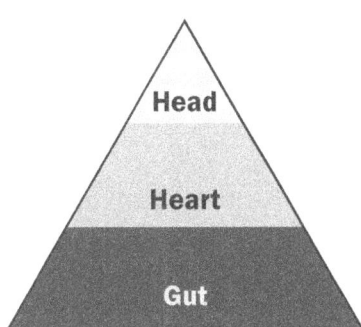

Based on coaching over 700 executives, however, I have seen that the most effective leaders trust their gut fully, and then bring their heart into the process and listen to it. They then use their heads to work out their logical next steps. This becomes a much easier, less stressful task because they've already chosen their course. Their three brains work together in harmony. When the three brains all work together, a leader is said to be a *complete leader,* and self-leadership is intact.[10]

Armed with this knowledge, I encourage you to begin observing yourself as you make decisions. What percentage of decisions do you make with your head, with your heart, and with your gut? Are you relying on one brain more than others? How could you vary your decision-making style, relying on your currently lesser-used brains more frequently? Balancing all three brains in decision-making will not only take the stress off of the brain you rely on the most, but will help you be a more complete self-leader in the process.

Your "Motivational Balance Sheet"

Here's another potential way to help you with decision-making. The "Motivational Balance Sheet" that follows allows you to look at the

---

10. Vikki Brock, EMBA, PhD, MCC, *Neuroscience and Coaching: Impact of Coaching on a Leader's Three Brains*, *Coaching Journal* (Dec. 2015), http://vikkibrock.com/wp-content/uploads/2014/05/UTD-Three-Brains-648efa8c-f301-4d1a-871b-5f4a09a315d7.pdf.

pros and cons of a situation and assess various possibilities by putting non-numerical choices into numerical terms. It sort of "levels the playing field" regardless of your industry, your background, or the way you view the world. In the process, you balance the head, heart, and gut, too.

Here's how it works: Let's say you're considering taking a different position within a new company. Write down all the key reasons (a) why you would take the job, and (b) why you would *not* want to take the job. To craft these two lists, listen to your head, your heart, and your gut.

Now, rate each of those reasons in terms of how important they are to you. Use a scale from 1 to 10, with "10" being very important to you, and "1" being not important at all. Then, simply add up your scores and see which list gets the highest number. Here's an example:

Motivational Balance Sheet— Accepting a Different Position in a New Company

Reasons to Accept	Importance Rating	Reasons *Not* to Accept	Importance Rating
I will make more money.	10	I will have to work longer hours.	9
I will experience exciting challenges.	8	There will be a learning curve, and I'll have to prove myself.	5
I will be more likely to reach my full potential.	10	It makes me nervous to make a change.	7
It would be good for my resume/CV.	8	I may end up with less time to spend with family.	10
Positive Total:	**36**	**Negative Total:**	**31**

In this case, the positives outscore the negatives, which might help you make the final decision.

Think of a tough choice you're facing right now, and use the Motivational Balance Sheet to help you make the decision. Are your gut, heart, and head brains all in alignment?

Heads or Tails?

Balance sheets like the one on the previous page are great when you have plenty of time to mull over possible outcomes. But what happens when you have to make a fast, tough decision, you don't seem to be getting a clear sense from your gut, and there's no time to do a full-fledged analysis?

In my coaching practice, I've found that the old "flip a coin" method can cut right through the confusion. Write down which of two possible decision outcomes will be "heads" and which will be "tails." Then, flip the coin, see how it lands, and *immediately* do a gut-and-heart check to gauge your feelings about that outcome. Are you disappointed with how the coin landed, or are you pleased? Often, this will tell you right away which decision is best.

Whichever method you use to make your choice, this is essential: Trust yourself. This is a cornerstone of self-leadership. Look inside, and know that you have exactly what you need to make a wise choice. You were put in your position of authority and responsibility for a good reason. If, for example, your decision involves letting someone go from your company (most often cited as one of the toughest "tough calls" a leader has to make), don't automatically assume that it will be a bad move for the employee. It might actually allow that person to find a new job that suits him or her better, and he/she she might even end up with a better-paying post, too.

The moral of the story: The consequences of making a tough decision aren't always what you expect, so if you find yourself feeling as if you're between a rock and a hard place, assume something good will come from the final choice you make. Even if the situation appears to turn out badly, you will have learned from the experience and strengthened your self-leadership in the process.

14

Limiting Self-Leadership Behavior #13:
Not Being Clear About Your Long-Term Career Aspirations

These are interesting times for leaders. Technology is changing the game every day, finding a good job can be difficult, and the international economic climate is as fickle as the weather in London. If you're like most executives, it's hard to find the time to sit down and contemplate where your career is going. But how can you be a good self-leader if you don't know exactly where you are leading yourself *to*?

It takes time and conscious effort to focus on your future, and most executives I've worked with have found that it's just easier to live from one moment to the next rather than make any kind of plan. But the truth is, if *you* don't make the time to determine your future, who will?

You're no longer at a level where you can leave your fate to "the powers that be" at headquarters or even to your immediate boss. If you wait for something outside of your control to change, you could end up waiting a very long time. So, in reality, there is nobody better than you to look at the big picture and set the direction for the next move in your career.

Take my client, Scott, as an example. A very successful lawyer in a large multinational firm, Scott hadn't taken the time to look at his career in a "big picture" way. Don't get me wrong—he was progressing up the ladder, and quite nicely at that—but not in a *strategic* way. He was simply moving along from job to job. He had no long-term perspective because he had gotten too caught up in each position's specific set of responsibilities and was only focusing on how to move forward to the next one. He had never thought about how each job could actually position him for much greater longer-term success.

Scott said to me (and I hear this a lot), "The truth is, Brenda, I've just been lucky all my career. The companies and opportunities have simply come to me; I didn't need to plan or strategize."

If this sounds familiar to you, I may know why. Early in your career, it isn't unusual for the next opportunity to just land in your lap. You produce, you deliver, and doing so results in more jobs and more opportunities appearing on the horizon.

But as you move up the ladder to increasingly senior positions, the number of jobs at that level diminishes. It becomes important to shift from being *re*active—simply choosing from among the various positions that are presented to you—to being *pro*active. When you are proactive, you ask yourself important questions that can change the trajectory of your professional life for the better: What do I really want long-term? Is my current position likely to lead me there? In order to reach my ultimate goal, what makes the most strategic sense for my career short-term, medium-term, and long-term?

As Laurence J. Peter, author of *The Peter Principle*, wrote: "If you don't know where you are going, you will probably end up somewhere else."

A Career with a View

It's one thing to say that you want to look at your career from a strategic vantage point, but it's another thing to actually do it.

To do this for Scott, he and I worked through what I call the "End-Point Exercise." You can try it, too:

1. First, draw a horizontal timeline with this year's date at the farthest-left end of the line. Then, reflect: At what age will you retire and/or quit working full-time? Be transparent with yourself. How many years do you honestly have remaining in your career? 10? 15? 20?

2. Write that retirement year at the furthest-right end on your timeline.

3. Then, ask yourself:
   - What does "success" look like at that final stage?
   - What do you want to be doing by then?
   - What is your ideal final post in this career of yours?

4. Spend some time visioning what your life will look like at that point. Don't limit your vision to your work life; think also about where you want to be with your family/personal life, community, spiritual life, philanthropy—all aspects of what is important to you.

Your "ideal" might be having the financial means to never have to—or want to—work again. Maybe you would like to take on an independent director board position, work part-time, or even start a business of your own, either for fun or for additional income. Your vision might include making sure you have enough money coming in for your children's university tuition and for your own retirement years. You might want to live in another country, spend more time with family, travel, or simply live the life you want as a happy, healthy retiree. But how do you make sure you get there?

This first step is key. You must be *crystal clear* in your mind about your "end game." Don't move forward with any other steps until you're absolutely certain that you have clarity about where you are headed.

To help you with this, I encourage you to create a vision for yourself. It can be a written narrative or a pictorial vision (with photos or magazine visuals that you pull together)—or it can be a combination of both. Be specific. You may want to talk about or develop your vision with your spouse or your significant other to assure that you have the same end game in mind.

Once you are crystal clear on the desired outcome, here's how to make this vision come to life: Envision that it is the last day of your work life. You've fast-forwarded to the year you've written at the farthest-right end of the timeline you drew.

Try it now. In your mind, imagine you are at your retirement party, and a big banquet has been organized in your honor. You are seated at the head table. All of your past and current coworkers are there to celebrate your life and career—your direct reports, peers, bosses, suppliers, and industry colleagues. Each individual stands up and pays tribute to you. What will they say about you in general? About what you did? About the specific contributions you made? About the kind of person you are? What would you like to hear them say as you sit there, listening to speech after speech?

Then, ask yourself this fundamental question: What will I need to do, and how will I need to be, to get to that point and deserve those accolades?

It helps to take a 360-degree approach to this exercise and look at the situation holistically:

- What character traits will you need to hone and polish?
- What specific skill sets will be key to your success?
- How much money will you need or want to have by then?
- What kinds of networks and connections will you require?

Create a list for yourself, and keep adding until you've written down all of the skills, attributes, and actions that you will need to get you to where you want to be.

Once that is clear, come back to the reality of today, and ask yourself: How would you rate yourself in each of those individual areas *now?* If the "end game" is a 10 (on a scale of 1 to 10, with 10 being high), how would you score yourself today in each specific area?

This assessment allows you to get crystal clear about (a) how well you are honestly doing now, and (b) where you will need to place the most focus between now and then. Which of your skills and talents need strengthening in order to achieve your goals by the end date? Get specific.

As I took Scott through the End-Point Exercise, he realized that he had aspirations to be a General Counsel in a large multinational corporation. That would involve carefully plotting his career to include new skills—both in the legal field and with people-leadership—that he hadn't previously considered. He would also need to network across other areas of the larger organization where he worked—within divisions where he hadn't made connections in the past. This prompted Scott to set up a series of lunches and coffees with various high-level leaders from other areas of the organization. It was a great example of getting proactive and taking self-leadership in career planning to a whole new level.

Matthew, another client, also completed the End-Point Exercise and realized that, after 25 years of working in global corporations, he wanted to experience some years as an entrepreneur once he retired from corporate life. Like Scott, Matthew had to reflect on the skills he would need in order to be a successful business owner as compared to working as an employee of other companies for so many years. This choice had important financial ramifications, too.

Another advantage of the End-Point Exercise is that it helps you break up your future into smaller, more manageable chunks of time. That, in turn, allows you to plan your self-leadership trajectory in an actionable and pragmatic way. You can tell yourself, "During 'this' particular period of time (e.g., Years 1-3), I will focus on developing 'this' specific skill and networking within the industry. Then, during the next period (Years 4-6), I will focus on developing 'these' other skills and networking across 'these' industries."

This is how you develop a concrete plan to plot your career strategically and make sure you're on track to end up where you want to be.

A Memorable Example of an Executive Who Made It Work

Does this kind of strategic planning work? Yes. Not only have I seen it work again and again in my Executive Coaching practice, but I was also exposed to this very early in my career— right out of business school— when I interviewed for a job at Procter & Gamble in Cincinnati.

At that time, applicants for brand management positions had to undergo three interviews by three potential colleagues and bosses. If you passed all three, you were given an employment offer. Each interview progressed higher up the corporate ranks, with the senior-most executive conducting the third interview.

I had apparently done well in all three interviews, but—for a variety of reasons—I wasn't all that excited about what I had seen or heard. So, in my head, I had decided this company and I were not a good match.

As I was leaving the third interview, however, I was summoned to the office of AG Lafley, who was at that time a Vice President in charge of a major division. (AG was eventually "kicked upstairs," serving both as P&G's CEO and as the Executive Chairman of the company's Board.)

In the short 45 minutes that I sat across the desk from AG, he convinced me to take the job—hook, line, and sinker! He was incredibly inspiring, and I remember his words very clearly, "You take care of this company, Brenda, and this company will take care of you." (They stuck to that, by the way.)

But beyond that, what was it that convinced me in such a short period to completely change my mind and sign on the dotted line? While AG and I were talking, he opened one of his desk drawers and pulled out a sheet of yellow-lined paper, which seemed to have been torn from a legal pad. It was his full, handwritten career plan, with one line devoted to each key post he wanted to attain and by when. You see, years before that, he had written his goals, outlined the skills he would need to learn, and highlighted the connections he would want to make. In short, he had laid out everything he would need to do to reach his personal and career goals for each year and as he moved forward.

I was incredibly impressed by AG's foresight which he had set down on paper so many years earlier. And I decided I wanted to work for someone like that, someone who was clearly a strong self-leader.

How about YOU™? If you're not yet clear about your desired career future, I encourage you to walk through the End-Point Exercise and begin to crystalize the end game. Where do you envision your career and your life taking you, and how will you get there?

15

Limiting Self-Leadership Behavior #14:
Not Knowing How to Influence Without Authority

Mei had just received a high-visibility promotion. It would take her from leading the sales function (with full profit & loss responsibility) to taking over a regional sales job in charge of 11 countries. However, with this new move, P&L responsibility would remain with the 11 country heads.

Her new regional job meant that there were dotted line reports in each of the 11 countries, but she had no "direct authority" over those reports or the country heads. She could no longer rely on an "I'm the boss" approach.

Mei came to me for coaching because she had never had a post which required her to rely solely on her ability to influence others; she had always relied on authority and title to get things done. As such, she felt the need to strengthen her influencing skills—and quickly—if she was going to succeed. Given the high visibility of her new position, not to mention how critical this was for her career, one thing was clear: Failure was not an option.

The need for greater influence skills is more and more common in today's matrixed world. Indeed, due to flattening organizations, so many executives today don't have the authority and positional power they previously had.

To further complicate matters, in today's global work world, the need to influence frequently happens *remotely*, with less face-to-face contact than in the past. That means we don't have the benefit of reading body language or using our facial expressions to help us persuade others to our point of view. Often, we have to speak to people in different time zones late at night or early in the morning, when we may be operating without the full energy we need.

As a result, influence is one of the most important skills of contemporary self-leadership, and that's why it's also one of the most common challenges I see in my executive coaching practice.

Assess Your Influence Skills

Is influence a "new" leadership topic? The enhanced need for it in today's world might make it appear to be, but if you stop and think about it, you've been influencing people since you were a baby. You cried to influence your mother to pick you up and hold you. You practiced influence strategies to get your parents to buy you the candy you wanted or to get a friend at school to choose you for a sports team. Maybe now you use your influence skills to convince your spouse to watch the movie you want to see. Influence is clearly a part of our ongoing lives.

But what is influence *really*? I like the definition that comes from the Center for Creative Leadership:

> *The power and the ability to personally affect others' actions, decisions, opinions, or thinking.*[11]

---

11. "Three Ways to Influence," *Center for Creative Leadership*, published March 24, 2016, http://insights.ccl.org/blog/three-ways-to-influence/.

Using this definition, take a moment right now and ask yourself: On a scale of 1 to 10, with 1 as low and 10 as high, how would you self-assess your influence level *internally*, i.e., within your organization?

Now, ask yourself the same question with regard to your influence *externally*, i.e., with clients and colleagues outside of your organization.

If you aren't particularly happy with the outcome of your assessment, don't worry. I'll share with you several ways to increase your influence that are authentic and which allow you to maintain your integrity. And even if you're already happy with your influence self-assessment scores, based on my coaching experience, there is almost always some room for improvement.

To start off your influence exploration, take a moment to reflect on who you need to influence in your professional life right now. Is it your boss, a peer, a coworker, or a client? What does success look like with this particular stakeholder? What would be the benefits of being able to influence this individual, and what are the consequences of *not* being able to influence him or her?

As an example, let's say employee turnover has been a big problem in your division, and you have a unique idea that you believe will promote retention. Your boss is reluctant to adopt the idea, however, because it's untried, and there is some risk and cost involved. You want to be able to influence your boss to see the advantages of your idea. You would personally benefit from your idea being implemented because it would mean your team members would spend less time training new employees. It would also be a feather in your cap professionally if the idea worked because it demonstrates out-of-the-box thinking, a skill you have on your personal development plan. And, of course, if you are not able to convince your boss to move your idea forward, you'll have to continue dealing with the stress of constant employee dissatisfaction and turnover.

Where do you start?

Relationships and Likability

I firmly believe that the effectiveness of your ability to influence directly correlates to the strength of your relationship with the person or persons you want to influence. Relationships are at the core of influence success, yet they are often overlooked.

Using the example mentioned in the last section, if you want to convince your boss to allow an employee retention strategy to be implemented, you will, quite simply, be more successful if you have a strong relationship with him or her.

With that in mind, pause and reflect on the state of your relationship with the person you identified as the individual you most want to influence. How would you assess that connection? Excellent? Good? Fair? Poor? What have you done to develop the relationship? What can you do to make it stronger?

Along these same lines, professors at Harvard Business School conducted a fascinating study that revealed the single most important key to influence. Can you guess what it is? Just for fun, I've offered up some choices below, the same choices I present to audiences when I speak at conferences about the topics of influence. Which answer do you think is correct?

Research by Harvard Business School reveals that _____ is the key to influence:

1. Having charisma

2. Demonstrating a sense of humor

3. Projecting warmth

4. Focusing on facts

5. Earning respect

Few of my program attendees get the answer right. The research reveals that the most important influencer is actually number 3: *Projecting warmth.*[12] Are you surprised?

According to that same study, leaders who score low on likability have about a *one in 2,000* chance of being regarded as effective. The researchers noted that while competence is important when it comes to influence, leaders should focus first on likability, which carries even more weight than competence.

It makes sense, right? Relationships, warmth, and likability. Influence is largely about how we feel and connect, and we're more willing to be persuaded by people we like and trust.

How Great Self-Leaders Influence

When you think about people who have a great deal of influence, does someone in your organization come to mind? What does this person do to influence others? Is the influence based solely on position and title, or is it based on a skill or quality like warmth and likability?

In the opening of this chapter, I mentioned my client, Mei, who struggled to influence, given that she no longer had direct authority. So, what happened? Even though she had never been forced to rely solely on influence before, I reminded her that she had certainly influenced her colleagues and others on a number of occasions. I asked her to make a list of ways that excellent self-leaders influence, recalling situations during her career in which she herself had successfully used influence, as well as times she had observed other great leaders influencing others.

Here is Mei's list:

- *"Great self-leaders influence by being fair and objective with others.* A number of my colleagues have reported to bosses who treated

---

12. Cuddy, Amy J.C.; Kohut, Matthew; Neffinger, John, "Connect, Then Lead," *Harvard Business Review,* July-August 2013, https://hbr.org/2013/07/connect-then-lead.

them unfairly at some point in their careers. That stays with you, and when you work with someone who *does* treat you fairly, you want to do right by that person.

- *Great self-leaders influence by having no hidden agendas.* It's important to be transparent. If people trust that I'm honest and up-front, they'll be more likely to accept what I have to say.

- *Great self-leaders influence peers by earning their respect.* If my peers don't respect me, I will be less likely to win them over.

- *Great self-leaders influence better when not attached to a specific outcome.* I'll be more influential if I stay flexible and don't insist that everything must be done in a certain way.

- *Great self-leaders influence by doing what's right for the team or the organization.* I need to keep in mind that it isn't personal; it's about doing what's best for the company.

- *Great self-leaders influence by asking powerful, open-ended questions.* These kinds of questions encourage dialogue, which, in turn, strengthens trust.

- *Great self-leaders influence by being inclusive, regardless of gender, race, ethnicity, age, or body type.* I need to watch any tendency toward unconscious bias and make sure I don't allow labels to negatively impact outcomes.

- *Great self-leaders influence by not overwhelming others with a lot of details.* I need to stay aware of how much information people actually need in order to see my point of view, and then offer no more than that.

- *Great self-leaders influence by steering clear of Drama and Problems.* I need to be positive and avoid complaining or focusing on what *isn't* working.

- *Great self-leaders influence by being excellent listeners.* My influence is more likely to be successful if I talk *with* people and listen actively rather than talking *at* them without listening."

Armed with these ideas and the Influence Toolbox in the next section, Mei felt more confident about her new position, and her previous trepidation about taking on the challenge turned to excitement.

What other examples have you seen great self-leaders use to successfully influence others?

The Influence "Toolbox"

While shadowing successful executives in the workplace, I've personally witnessed a number of influence strategies. Using that experience, I've created my own customized "Influence Toolbox," which also incorporates some key principles from two existing influence models.[13]

In the Toolbox, there are three main categories, which all have "building relationships" at the center.

1. Logical

2. Emotional

3. Collaborative

Within those three categories of the Influence Toolbox (illustrated on the following page) are 12 different influencing tactics that you can use. These are hardly exhaustive, but they are the 12 tactics that I have seen used most effectively to influence at work.

Notice in the Influence Toolbox that the 12 strategies are not evenly distributed between the three categories. You might think that influence tactics in the Logical category would be plentiful, but in my opinion, there are only three worth exploring, while the Emotional and Collaborative categories contain five and four tactics, respectively.

---

13. Models from the Center for Creative Leadership and Robert Cialdini's Influence Principles.

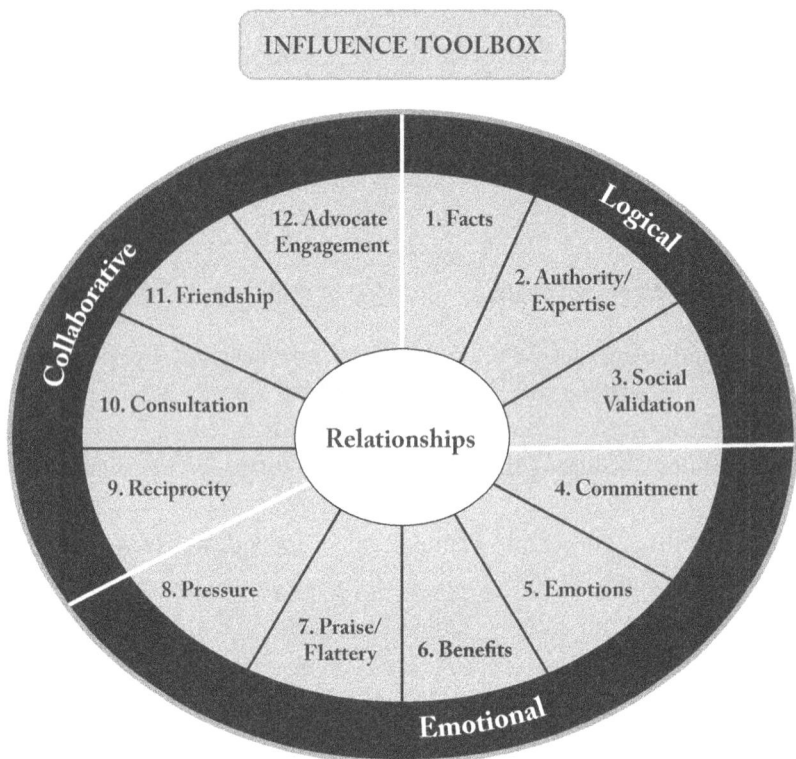

Let's take a look at each of these tools that you can use to influence others.

Logical:

1. **Facts.** This includes the use of factual data that might convince someone to see your point of view. While we've already established that facts are not as powerful as warmth and likability, it's still a great tool to use in certain situations. For example, you might say, "We should explore developing this new product because our #1 client in India and our #2 client in China said they would benefit from it."

2. **Authority/Expertise.** In this case, you influence others by offering the opinion of an expert or authority on the subject. "The head of M&A agrees that we should move forward with this negotiation," is an example of using authority to influence.

3. **Social Validation.** You can sometimes convince others to your side if you show that someone else is successfully using a similar idea. For example: "Our two top competitors use this IT system, so I think we should, too."

Emotional:

4. **Commitment.** Others are more willing to agree with your perspective if they see your personal commitment to it. If team members see you working on a project late at night or early in the morning, for example, they will witness how committed you are and will likely increase their own commitment to your point of view.

5. **Emotions.** Passion, empathy, and trust are examples of powerful emotional influencers. When people see that you're passionate about something, they will be much more likely to agree with you. Similarly, if you empathize with the individuals you are trying to influence, you'll likely earn their trust. You can do this by putting yourself in the other person's shoes and trying to understand his or her experience.

6. **Benefits.** In this case, you point out what's in it for the person you're trying to influence. For example, "You'll grow your business by 10% by using this new product," or "Your employees will be more engaged if you implement this protocol."

7. **Praise and Flattery.** I find coaching clients often resist this tool because they feel it's disingenuous, but the truth is that we use praise and flattery quite frequently. Think about it: Haven't you used flattery on occasion to gain someone's favor? Keep in mind that it needs to be real and heartfelt, and *how* you do it is critical, too. For example, you could say, "I genuinely applaud you for the business you've built—I'm impressed! And, I believe our firm can help you take it to the next level."

8. **Pressure.** This is a tool most coaching clients swear they never use. But then, I challenge them by saying, "I wonder if the people who work with you would see it that way?" That comment usually evokes a chuckle. The truth is that we all use pressure from time

to time to influence others. For example: "I need it by tomorrow at 8:00 a.m. sharp, no questions asked!" It's an emotional strategy that evokes fear and, while it can be intimidating, it can also be highly effective when used appropriately—albeit sparingly!

Collaborative:

9. **Reciprocity.** This is the classic "I'll scratch your back if you scratch mine" tactic. If you aren't familiar with that expression, it means that if the person you want to influence will agree to what you want, you will do something for that same person in return. For example: "If you can get me the report by Friday morning, I'll make sure your hard work is showcased," or "If you could just move the board meeting by one day, I can get back in time to be there and support you."

10. **Consultation.** In this case, you ask the person you want to influence to be part of the solution, which is likely to persuade him or her to get involved. For example, you might say to a client, "I'd appreciate your advice on the plan for our new product launch. What do you think would be the best way to interest customers in buying it?" This is a smart way to not only get great ideas for how to solve challenges, but to get others engaged in helping with the outcome.

11. **Friendship.** We tend to support and agree with people we like most. If you have invested time in becoming a genuine friend and have enjoyed social times with those you want to influence, you'll have a better chance of gaining their cooperation on key issues.

12. **Advocate Engagement.** This tactic involves asking others to help you engage with the people you want to persuade. Advocate engagement is all about making connections to reach out to and impact your influence target. Think of it as the "LinkedIn of influence!" For example, if you know someone who's closely connected with the person you want to influence, get that person engaged in helping you to influence the target.

Now that you've read about the various ways to influence someone, reflect and consider: Which three of the Toolbox techniques do you currently use most often? Which ones are in your comfort zone? Which three do you use least often? Which ones, if any, are completely untried or unfamiliar to you?

We tend to get stuck using only those strategies that have worked for us in the past, but I call this resource the Influence "Toolbox" because all of these ideas are readily available to you. If you want to have more influence, it's important to use a mixture of these tools—to "vary it up." That way, you can choose what you believe will work best with the particular stakeholder you want to impact.

By developing your agility in using a variety of these tools, you can pick the appropriate method in the moment. You can even combine them. For example, you might use Facts, along with Commitment, Benefits, Friendship, and Reciprocity. Of course, you don't have to overcompensate and pile on too many strategies at once, but if one doesn't work, you can be prepared with others.

Choose one or two strategies to work on, and once you feel you have a handle on those, move on to a couple more until you have filled your own Influence Toolbox with all twelve.

Resistance, Compliance, or Commitment?

Whatever influence strategy you employ, the Center for Creative Leadership outlines three possible outcomes, which I imagine we have all seen playing out in our work worlds:

1. **Resistance.** In this case, the person you want to influence isn't on board at all and refuses to agree with your point of view. In fact, they may even push back on the idea and/or intentionally fight against it.
2. **Compliance.** This outcome occurs quite often. The individual you're trying to influence says, "Yes, I'll do it." That person will

seemingly do whatever he or she has agreed to do, but has no genuine dedication to your desired outcomes.

3. **Commitment.** This, of course, is the ultimate outcome of influence—enthusiastic agreement and a true commitment to move forward with what you want. The more you use the strategies and tips in this chapter, the more likely you'll be able to obtain genuine commitment from those you want to persuade.

Consider someone you are currently trying to influence at work. Which of the strategies in this chapter do you think would work best for this particular stakeholder, given the situation? Which would most likely instill true commitment from him or her? Remember that you can combine tools. If you choose a few and give them a try, you may be surprised by the power of your influence.

16

Limiting Self-Leadership Behavior #15:
Failing to Seek Regular and "Real" Feedback

Management guru Ken Blanchard often quotes his friend, Rich Case, as saying, "Feedback is the breakfast of champions." If that is the case, how often and how well are YOU™ being fed?

If you're like most leaders I've met, you aren't getting enough regular feedback. That's why the best self-leaders ask for feedback regularly. If no one is offering you feedback because of your heightened position, or if you don't feel you're getting honest feedback, you have to take the initiative to go after it. You have to make sure that you get feedback some way, somehow. There's simply no better way to excel in your current position and accelerate your career.

Of course, asking for feedback may not be something you love doing. Let's face it: It can be somewhat painful to learn about your shortcomings, even if there are only relatively small issues that need improvement. But the other reality to face is that *not* accepting criticism can cause your career to come to a crashing halt. So, it becomes a matter of trading off the long-term pain of a career that isn't reaching its full potential for the short-term potential pain of a little constructive criticism. That feedback could ultimately help you move forward and perhaps even help you reach heights beyond what you thought possible.

Once you know what needs improvement, you're then armed with the information you need to move forward. There's a certain excitement that comes from developing your self-leadership skills and getting better at your job. It's almost always guaranteed to rejuvenate you and give you renewed energy in your position … if you let it.

Why Don't Leaders Seek More Feedback?

Despite the known benefits of getting input from others, too many executives continue as usual without getting enough feedback about their performance. Why is that? These are the five main reasons I've seen. Do you recognize yourself in any of these?

1. *As you climb higher, you become less coachable.* Highlighting what P&G's former CEO John Pepper said, the higher up you get, the easier it can be for you to think you've learned all you need to know. One of the U.S.'s founding fathers, Thomas Jefferson, said it well: "He who knows most, knows how little he knows." Even the highest-level leaders—or, more accurately, *especially* the highest-level leaders—must not only be open to hearing feedback, but must regularly seek it out.

2. *You let your ego/pride stop you from getting feedback.* Perhaps you believe that getting feedback from your direct reports will make you look weak. You fear you'll appear flawed or that your effectiveness will be undermined if you ask for suggestions. Remember that, even though you're the boss, you're still human, and it's all right to be seen that way.

3. *You're concerned that the feedback you do get won't be genuine.* It's possible that no one wants to endanger their job by telling you (the boss) what you're doing wrong or which decisions won't work.

It's true that most subordinates may not be fully truthful about the downsides of working with senior leaders; otherwise, they fear the boss might hold perceived negative feedback against them. This, of course, negates the entire purpose of giving feedback in the first place! But there are definitely a few ways that you can get accurate feedback from subordinates and others. We'll explore some of those ways later in this chapter.

4. *The feedback received doesn't come from the right people.* Feedback for high-level execs may come from board members or other high-level leaders who don't work closely or that often with you, so their remarks may not reflect the reality of what it's like to work with you every day. If feedback is to be helpful, it should come from the individuals who work very closely with you, who understand the ins and outs of your job, and who most frequently see you in action.

5. *You're content to just continue on as you've always done, as long as nothing appears to be wrong.* You may feel you're doing fine, so why stir things up by asking how you can improve, right? But, one of the worst things we can do in our careers or in life is just sit back and become complacent. "Checking out mentally" is the opposite of self-leadership—it won't get you anywhere.

The Do's and Don'ts of Feedback

The bottom line: It's critical at all levels of an organization to get feedback from others. Here are some do's and don'ts that will help you get helpful feedback you can truly use:

Do make it clear to feedback providers that you're sincere and want their remarks to be honest. Encourage them to be candid, and let them know that's exactly the kind of input you're looking for.

Do ask for feedback from coworkers at different levels within the organization—your boss, your subordinates, key peers, and colleagues. They might have different perspectives on your work and your behaviors, so getting all of their opinions will help you see a variety of viewpoints from a "surround-sound" perspective. That can help you grow in various ways.

Do say "thank you" when someone shares feedback with you—and that's all you need to say, whether you agree with what you heard or not. This holds especially true if they offered perceived "negative" inputs. If you're not the sort of person who's good at taking criticism, there's nothing wrong with "rehearsing" ahead of time. Try to anticipate the things people might tell you, and prepare yourself emotionally to react well. You don't need to commit to making a change on the spot; you can decide what to do with the feedback later. Just thank them, genuinely, and remember that they've given you information you can use. See it as a gift.

Do listen closely, and take notes on what is said. Don't try to remember your feedback providers' remarks in your head because if you're feeling any emotion or anxiety, no matter how prepared you think you are, your mind will likely get cluttered. Plus, when the person sees you writing down their remarks, they'll be convinced you really *are* sincere about getting honest feedback. And it will be helpful, later, to have your notes in front of you as you review the inputs and plan what to do with them.

Do devise an anonymous questionnaire if you think you might not get genuine feedback any other way. Again, those who hold very top positions may find it difficult to persuade subordinates to speak with honesty or to criticize "the boss" in any way. Your own comfort level might even be enhanced if you can ask questions in writing. Design the questions in whatever format will suit your purposes: You can write questions that require simple "Yes" or "No" answers, or those that rate you on a scale of 1-6 or 1-10. Or you can combine these styles, even asking a few "narrative" questions, e.g., to write a sentence or a paragraph in response. You'll be able to see which types of questions bring the most useful information and remember that for future surveys.

Do hire a coach to interview selected colleagues and subordinates if you think those feedback providers might be too intimidated to give you straightforward inputs directly. Have the coach assure the feedback providers that their comments will be kept completely anonymous. Their responses will almost certainly be more forthright if they know that no one will share "who said what" with the feedback recipient.

Do create questions that correspond to specific key self-leadership qualities or skills that you want to improve. Here are a few suggestions—you can pick and choose—but always try to start off with "positive" input questions (e.g., the first two below) as people are generally open to sharing "negative" inputs once they've had a chance to share positives first.

- What would you say are the top three things I'm doing well?
- In general, what should I continue doing?
- What would you like me to start doing?
- What would you like me to stop doing?
- What do I do too much?
- What do I do too little?
- What do you need from me that I haven't been providing?
- How could I communicate better?
- What could I do to help improve overall productivity?
- If you were in my position, what would you suggest I do differently from what I'm doing now?

If you aren't sure which questions are relevant, you might explain self-leadership to them. Then, simply ask, "What are 2-3 most important ways I could lead myself better?" Or, "How can I lead myself differently in order to become a better boss/co-worker/colleague/subordinate?"

Don't make your request too open-ended by saying something like, "Give me feedback, please." People won't know what to say, and they'll likely be lost trying to figure out what you're looking for. But if you ask them specific questions, like from the list above, you will likely end up with very useful inputs that can drive tangible strategies for improving your performance and strengthening your self-leadership skills.

Don't ask for feedback from colleagues or direct reports when they are in a group. I once witnessed a CEO who did this. Instead of asking his staff for feedback one-on-one, he surprised them in a group meeting with the question, "Okay, let's get it out on the table now: How am I doing?" Later, many of the direct reports told me they felt "ambushed." They were blindsided by the question and felt that the boss was putting them on the spot. Most of them glanced down at their hands and said nothing. Only one person in the meeting had the courage to tell the CEO what he thought, and guess what happened to that individual? The boss held a grudge against him and didn't treat him fairly from that moment on.

Don't get defensive, no matter what kind of feedback you get. You've asked people to be honest with you (and you *did* mean it, right?), so if you don't accept the criticism gracefully, there's a good chance they will never offer honest feedback again. Just think about the CEO in the above example—if you had been in that meeting, can you imagine *ever* offering him honest feedback again? No way. So, he will become yet another C-Suite executive who will never find out what people really think of him, simply because he was too insecure to accept genuine criticism. Of course, that kind of insecurity goes strongly against the grain of self-leadership. It's extremely important to train yourself to stay silent and listen actively while receiving feedback.

You Have Your Feedback—Now What?

Once you've gathered feedback, look for patterns and themes. For instance:

- Do others tell you you're too negative, pessimistic, or defensive at work, implying that you may be demonstrating a victim mindset?

- Were you told that you tend to avoid—or cause—conflict within the organization?

- Did more than one person tell you that you don't listen as well as you could?

- Does your feedback indicate that you're often late, showing that you could improve your time management skills?

Write down the main themes you find in the criticisms. Then, reflect, and write down the behaviors that create these themes.

If you don't feel you can figure out how to improve the behaviors uncovered by the feedback themes, ask someone from Human Resources, enlist a trusted colleague, discuss with a trusted mentor, or find a coach to guide you through the changes you want to make.

Once you become more comfortable with feedback, my hope is that you grow to love it. When the comments are productive, they give you a chance to genuinely improve your performance and reach goals that you might never have thought you could achieve. That's what strong self-leadership is all about.

17

Setting Self-Leadership Goals

We've now explored all 15 self-leadership behaviors that might be standing in the way of advancing your career. As you review these again, reflect on the top three you do best and the three you would like to improve the most:

- Believing you're a victim at work
- Not managing your mind
- Getting stuck in black-and-white thinking
- Devoting little or no time to strategic thinking
- Ignoring the importance of time management
- Saying "yes" when you want to say "no"
- Failing to address conflict when it arises
- Not being ready for the challenges of today's diverse workplace
- Managing down more than up and across

- Overlooking the importance of Executive Presence

- Underestimating the significance of self-promotion and visibility

- Struggling with tough decisions

- Not being clear about your long-term career aspirations

- Not knowing how to influence without authority

- Failing to seek regular and "real" feedback

Setting Goals to Create New Positive Behavior Habits

Most leaders know the power of setting goals, but one of the best examples of this, I think, rests with arguably the most successful professional basketball player in history: Michael Jordan.

Jordan's accolades go on and on. He was National Basketball Association scoring champion 10 times, NBA All-Star 14 times, NBA Finals Most Valuable Player 6 times, and is the scoring record-holder for the Chicago Bulls. And that's just the tip of the iceberg.

But was he always that successful? No. In fact, as a sophomore in high school, Michael Jordan was such a poor basketball player that he was cut from the varsity team. Jordan was crushed, and that turned out to be a defining moment for the now-legend.

As Jordan tells it, "I knew I never wanted to feel that bad again." So, he decided to set a goal of being a starter on the varsity team. He focused on that goal all summer. Whenever he practiced, "that's what I thought about," he said. He worked extremely hard to earn a spot on the varsity team. And he did.

This started a habit of goal-setting for Jordan. "I approach everything step by step," he has said. "I always set short-term goals, and each one of the steps or successes led to the next one."

After he made the team, he set another goal—"a reasonable, manageable goal that I could realistically achieve if I worked hard enough." He continued to practice constantly, and he made his next goal. He kept setting goals, each building on the last and working hard to make each accomplishment happen. "I gained a little confidence every time I came through," and he always kept the end in mind. "I knew where I wanted to go. Step by step—I can't see any other way of accomplishing anything," he said.[14]

Of course, very few of us will become basketball legends, but we can all use a goal-setting process in order to succeed. And we can focus, practice, and work hard to make each one a reality. Each time we set a goal, it serves multiple purposes:

- It creates commitment, the backbone of self-leadership.
- It gives you focus.
- It keeps you motivated.
- It challenges you to grow.

Combine those four purposes, and they add up to the kind of future you want as a self-leader who's determined to succeed and knows how to get there.

Think about a past goal you set for yourself—did you succeed at it? Did you fail? Regardless of the outcome, what did you learn about yourself in the process?

With those answers in mind, choose the first of the 15 self-leadership behaviors you would like to focus on, and make it your next goal. Once you've reached that milestone, choose the next important behavior to master, and make that your second self-leadership goal. Eventually, you can work on all 15 behaviors, as need be.

---

14. Jordan, Michael and Vancil, Mark, *I Can't Accept Not Trying: Michael Jordan on the Pursuit of Excellence,* (HarperCollins, 1994).

Word Your Goals Carefully

When establishing your goals, be careful how you word them. Here are a few missteps I often see in the goal-setting process and a few guidelines for how to avoid them:

Proposed Goal: "I want the people I work with to be more …"
Why this won't work: Your goal should be about *you* and *your* self-leadership desires—not those of your peers, colleagues, boss, or team members.

Proposed Goal: "When I speak, I don't want to sound apologetic …"
Why this won't work: It isn't focused on the positive. Train yourself to replace negative talk with positives, such as, "Every time I engage with senior management, I speak with confidence."

Proposed Goal: "I will prepare for two hours before each presentation …"
Why this won't work: This is an example of *how* you will achieve your goal —so, it's a strategy; it doesn't specify what your goal is. A related goal might be: "I consistently present with poise and confidence."

30 Days to a New YOU™

Changes can take place quickly if you're determined, but your current, ingrained behaviors are habits that most likely took years to become entrenched. So, it's important to identify when you indulge in those specific behaviors. Then, you'll become more aware of how—and how quickly—you can change them.

Studies tell us that it takes at least 21 days to turn a new behavior into a habit if you work on it every day. Since the average month has about 22 working days, I suggest a 30-day plan to instill your first new self-leadership habit. Within 30 days, if you're giving it your best effort, you—and those around you—should expect to see progress.

After you've worked on your goal for 30 days, meet one-on-one again with everyone who gave you feedback, or ask them to fill out your questionnaire again. Ask if they've seen any improvements; if so, what specifically did they notice?

As I've said, if you are someone who hasn't enjoyed feedback in the past, that's likely to change. You'll soon discover how rewarding self-improvement and real self-leadership can be. You're changing long-ingrained habits, and with every step in the right direction, there comes a sense of accomplishment. Plus, the newfound respect from work colleagues, after they see you truly listened to their feedback and acted on it, will be invaluable. They'll see you as a role model for coachability and how to use feedback for professional development.

Going to the "M-A-T" for Your Goals

Setting goals is one thing, but they won't do you much good if you're not motivated to work toward them. A lot of executives make elegant plans, but aren't enthusiastic enough to move forward—what I call "being in inaction."

Many of us struggle to get going. You can be a terrific leader with a great idea, but it will remain an idea and nothing more if you don't propel yourself to act on it.

This exercise can help you gauge your motivation level. I call it the "M-A-T Model," adapted from the Fogg Behavior Model developed at Stanford University. The intention behind the exercise is to help form a new habit. Begin by thinking of the behavior that you've now chosen as your first self-leadership goal.

> **M** – **Motivation.** On a scale of 1 to 10, with 10 as the highest score, rate how *motivated* you are to change this specific self-leadership behavior and establish a new positive habit. If your score is 8 or

lower, that may not be enough to catapult you to where you want to be. Pause before you move to the next step. Remind yourself of the benefits you'll enjoy once you reach this goal. Keep those benefits in mind, and don't move on to the next step until you can honestly give your motivation a score of 9 or 10. Then, you're truly ready to embrace change.

A – Ability. These are the tips, tools, and techniques that you'll use to create your new habit and reach your goal—the types of suggestions that are in this book. Which information or resources will help you the most? Keep applying the tools and practicing until you reach your goal.

T – Trigger. To remind you of your goal and keep it top of mind, you can use a catalyst—an image or a symbol—to recall the goal every time you see it. One client has a map of the world on her wall, reminding her that she isn't working just to pay the bills. She wants enough savings to take her extended family on an around-the-world trip. Another carries a small pebble in his pants pocket—a pebble that comes from the property of a small villa he owns by a beach—as a reminder of the work/life balance he's seeking. What trigger can you use to remind yourself of your first self-leadership goal?

Goal, Strategy, or Action?

Once you establish your first goal, you want to develop strategies and actions to help you get there. A fair number of leaders aren't all that clear about the difference between a goal, a strategy, and an action, though, so let me share a metaphor.

Pretend that you're standing on a tiny island in the middle of a large body of water. What you want to achieve (the *goal* you have defined above) is located on the bank on the opposite side of the water. To get to your goal, you will have to swim to that other bank. There's just one problem: The water is shark-infested. How will you safely cross the water to get there?

As it turns out, there are large rocks sticking out of the water, located between you and that opposite shore, each rock lined up and symbolizing a key milestone you need to reach in order to eventually get to your goal. Those are your *strategies*.

Between each large rock is an imaginary arrow, and the arrows symbolize the specific *actions* you'll take to move you along from one milestone to the next.

As you reach each milestone, be sure to celebrate having achieved yet another step toward your self-leadership goal. Reminding yourself that you are making progress will motivate you to keep going.

Get clear on your goals, your strategies, and your actions. And, remember what Mahatma Gandhi said: "You may never know what results come of your action, but if you do nothing, there will be no result."

Accountability—The Final Key

I also recommend enlisting an "accountability buddy" to hold you bound and focused on reaching your goal. This could be a colleague, friend, spouse, or external coach who helps keep you on track.

Not convinced of the value of an accountability partner? One study released by Dominican University of California found that people were 33% more successful in reaching their stated goals when they sent weekly updates to a boss or colleague.

Even more telling: In his book, *It's Not About the Money*, Bob Proctor quotes a Brigham Young University study about people trying to change some aspect of their lives. He reports:

- Those who stated, "That's a good idea," had only a 10% chance of actually making a change.
- Those who committed and said, "I'll do it," had a 25% chance of making a change.

- Those who said *when* they would take action showed a 40% chance of making a change.

- Those who set a specific plan of *how* to do it had a 50% chance of making a change.

- Those who committed to *someone else* that they would do it had a 60% chance of making a change.

- And those who set a *specific time to share their progress with someone else* had a 95% chance of making a change.

Your accountability partnership has the best chance of succeeding if you reciprocate and help the other person achieve his or her goals as well. Make a schedule with due dates for tasks, and as you work toward completing each specific one, check in with your accountability partner to stay motivated. On a regular basis, ask what the other needs from you, and be sure you know the best ways to motivate each other. If you come across challenges or obstacles on your way to your goals, talk openly about them.

In the meantime, celebrate together when you meet your goals, congratulate yourselves on your progress, and keep at it. With each step you take, you'll strengthen your self-leadership and further build your Executive Leadership Brand.

18

Leading YOU™ to Success

We've all heard the saying, "It's lonely at the top." There's definitely some truth to that—it's just the sheer nature of the beast as you climb higher up the corporate staircase. At this level, everyone you turn to for advice or feedback may seem to have a hidden agenda. No matter how hard they may try, their perspectives can't help but be biased. This includes your spouse, your children, your boss, your Board of Directors, your subordinates, and your peers.

It's not that you can't trust these individuals, or that they don't like you or respect you. It's just that the higher you get and the more power you have, the more colleagues start seeing you as a key connection "at the top." They need an ally in your position if they want to make things happen, so it may be difficult for them to talk to you with full transparency.

As many executives have told me, each time you get promoted, you have fewer and fewer people you can turn to for open, honest, no-strings-attached advice and counsel. As we discussed in Chapter 16, effective self-leadership depends on getting genuine feedback, as well as being able to see the big picture, and you simply cannot see everything from the corner office.

My client, Peter, had this problem. He was a senior leader in a large organization. When he got promoted to CEO, he told me that everything changed overnight. The people he previously had turned to for advice and counsel—or even for a short "chat" at lunchtime—suddenly seemed to look at him differently. He told me he felt the energy shift. People were not as forthcoming or as straightforward as they had been before he was "kicked upstairs." It was as if he suddenly was living in a bubble, with all eyes focused on him.

Peter likewise told me that every move he made at that level was amplified. "If I sneeze," he said, "I feel as if the entire organization will catch a cold. I have to watch every move so carefully." As we discussed in the chapter about visibility, moving up the ladder can sometimes make you feel as if you are living and working in a fishbowl.

In the chapter on feedback, I shared how it can be more challenging to get honest inputs at the higher levels of an organization. Why does that happen? Here are a few scenarios that could lend some insight behind this issue:

- Your peers and colleagues are suddenly more conscious of the potential consequences of being straightforward with you. Knowing that you have full power over their positions and decisions can be intimidating to some of them. Let's face it: How much can you speak openly about the "ugly truth" of what's going on in the company without fear of recrimination from the highest-level leaders?

- Previous confidantes now want to demonstrate to others that you—a high-level leader—trust them because that, in turn, raises *their* power and clout within the organization. As a result, they may end up sharing information with others that you specifically asked them to keep private.

- You are now privy to more confidential information than ever before, yet there are fewer and fewer people with whom you can discuss it. The decisions you must make involve not only individuals and teams, but the entire organization, and it would be helpful to bounce your thoughts off of someone—but it all has to be kept quiet. Who can you turn to?

- You don't want to confide "up" to the most senior leaders or board members, for fear they'll judge you and think it was a mistake to put you in this powerful position in the first place. High-level people are supposed to be able to think for themselves and make the right decisions, correct?

- You don't want to turn to peers because they might also have been in the running for your current position. As a result, there could be some hard feelings or, at the very least, discomfort.

If any of these scenarios sound familiar to you, you might resort to believing it's just best to "go it alone." You might even have already tried that. But, no two people can see things in the same way, so again, outside perspectives are simply required for good self-leadership *and* effective leadership of your company, your division, your function, or your team.

Where Can Senior Leaders Find Impartial Advice?

Given all of this, where can you turn for objective opinions? Here's a brief example from my own experience: When I first went to work for Procter & Gamble, like any new recruit, I started in an entry-level position. Remember my story about AG Lafley, the Vice President of our division (who later became P&G's Chairman and CEO)? He gave me the great advice about thinking big-picture about my career. He had personally recruited me from Harvard Business School, which was also his alma mater, so he had gotten to know me from the hiring process. Still, I was surprised when he would occasionally make a trip "downstairs" to chat with me. He would pull up a chair and ask questions such as, "How is morale within the division?" and "What's the latest news inside the organization?"

I always enjoyed those chats but didn't understand why AG would spend so much time with someone like me, whose position was many levels below his. So, one evening when I was working late and he stopped by, I asked him what he got out of our talks.

"That's simple," he replied. "The higher you get in the organization, the harder it is to get pure, unfiltered information. I knew the minute I recruited you that you would be a straight shooter. I knew you would give me honest answers about what's happening at the ground level." That conversation not only cleared up a mystery for me, but it also provided an important lesson about getting feedback as a senior leader.

But what if you don't have a trusted "straight shooter" within your organization that you can rely on? Executive coaching may be the answer.

There's an unfortunate myth about executive coaching that it's only about "fixing problems," but nothing could be further from the truth. Coaching isn't consulting, counseling, or therapy. It isn't about regretting a past that can't be changed. It's about focusing on a future that *can* be changed. Executive coaching helps already successful leaders achieve even more as they progress.

An executive coach is a skilled professional who develops an ongoing relationship with you and focuses on helping you take action toward realizing your stated goals. A good coach doesn't provide you with solutions. Instead, the coach draws out solutions from *you*. This helps you achieve positive, lasting changes in behavior that transform yourself and your team/organization. This, of course, leads to skillful self-leadership and better outcomes overall.

Think about the original definition of the word "coach." It was a vehicle, usually horse-drawn, that took someone from one place to another. That is what a good executive coach does: The coaching process is a means of helping you get from where you are now to where you want to be. And the harsh truth is that the skills that supported you in getting your current position may not be enough to advance higher up, or even keep you competitive at your new level. The game has changed considerably in the last 25-30 years, and a coach can help you make sure you stay a top player.

Why the Work World Needs Executive Coaches: A Bit of Corporate History

In the 1970s and 1980s, corporations were built based on a "tall" pyramid structure with the CEO at the top and multiple levels below that. At each level, leaders usually only had three to five direct reports. Each leader was tasked with grooming his or her subordinates and was able to provide plenty of one-on-one time to do that. The focus was on developing *functional* skills during that era—marketing, finance, operations, and sales—and, as long as you had strong skills in one particular area, you could continue to rise up the corporate ladder and win as a leader. Those functional capabilities were termed "hard" skills, while "soft" skills, such as team management and self-leadership, were considered less important.

Then the 1990s arrived, and Wall Street got tougher on companies, demanding consistently better results. Around the world, markets had tapped out domestically so corporations actively started looking overseas for opportunities. This brought about a surge of mergers and acquisitions, not just domestically but globally. As a result, extremely large organizations began to take form, and these huge conglomerates were simply too big for a tall pyramid structure to work.

So, organizations became "flatter," cutting out many levels, leaving leaders with many more direct reports than before—to the tune of eight to 15 or even more, as we see today. These organizations also took on a matrixed structure, so leaders began to have multiple bosses across the organization—for example, one functional leader and one geographic leader. All of this resulted in much less one-on-one time with any boss, leaving behind the hand-held leadership development of the past.

To make things even more interesting, during this same period, more women entered the workplace while more global mergers brought greater cultural diversity to work environments. And as we know from the chapter on unconscious bias, for the first time in the history of humankind, four generations are now working under the same roof due to longer life spans and individuals choosing to work well into their 60s, 70s, and even 80s.

Bottom line: In the last 30+ years, organizations have become more complicated, creating the need for new skills, particularly the ability to maneuver through these complicated work landscapes. This requires more *interpersonal* skills—those previously labeled "soft" self-leadership abilities that took a backseat to more tangible "hard" or functional skills.

In this new environment, what used to be called "hard" skills have become the price of entry. It is now *expected* that you will quickly figure out the functional requirements of your job. In their place, it's the "soft" skills that are becoming so critical to success today. Despite this fact, flattened organizations allow little or no time for busy leaders to receive or provide direct on-the-job coaching. Likewise, universities rarely teach the kind of hands-on interpersonal skills you need at work, so leaders aren't always adequately trained to handle the challenges of self- and team-management.

Due in part to this lack of one-on-one, on-the-job skills development, employee loyalty has dropped dramatically. The average tenure at a typical job today is about 3–4 years ... and getting shorter. Employers are finding it more and more difficult to retain their best staff. The pace of change is relentless and also includes a heightened regulatory environment for many industries. There's more scrutiny on all fronts now, too, which brings added stress and pressure. As the last of the Baby Boomers (one of the largest groups ever in the workforce) reach retirement age, there will be an even greater shortage of good leaders.

You can see now why, in a study of CEOs in North America, Europe, and Asia, 91% revealed that "developing leaders" is the most critical success factor for growth in today's work world.

Executive Coaching is On the Rise

With all of that fast and furious change, no wonder executive coaching is more common these days, especially with top executives expressing such a need to develop strong leaders. In a *Fortune* 500 survey, 43% of CEOs and 71% of senior executive teams said they have worked with a coach, 63% of companies said they plan to increase their use of coaching over the next five years, and 92% of leaders who have used a coach in the past say they plan to do so again.

Why such an investment in coaching? Simply put, statistics show that it pays off! In a study of 370 participants who had worked with executive coaches, the group went from the 50th percentile in performance to the 93rd percentile. Amoco Corp/BP assessed the impact of executive coaching over a 10-year period and discovered that managers who were coached received 50% higher average salary increases.

What Can a Coach Do for YOU™?

Executives turn to coaching for help in a range of diverse areas. A survey of executive coaches revealed the top three reasons that leaders engage them:

- 48% said it was to develop high-potential employees or facilitate a transition.
- 26% said leaders wanted an objective sounding board.
- 12% said leaders wanted to address derailing behaviors.

Here are some of the other top reasons that executives turn to coaching:

- Develop stronger leadership skills/core competencies.
- Transition successfully into a new position.
- Achieve greater overall business success.
- Implement a new strategy, vision, or direction.

- Create a more positive workplace environment.
- Determine a career strategy.
- Reduce/better manage stress.
- Improve time management and work/life balance.
- Foster better self-coaching behaviors.
- Develop conflict management skills.

What to Look for in an Executive Coach

You are probably aware that engaging an executive coach can be a great personal and professional move, but how do you choose the right coach for you? First and foremost, do your research: Ask colleagues and others who have worked with coaches for referrals. Search for experienced coaches online. Ask to see training certificates, and read testimonials. There are many assessment trainings that are important for a coach to have completed, but they often include names and acronyms such as Extended DISC, Hogan, MBTI, FIRO-B, LPI, EQI, or CPI.

A good executive coach understands both business operations *and* human behavior. The best coaches have been business leaders themselves and know how to maneuver their way through the inner workings of an organization. Yet, they also understand how behaviors can spell either success or failure. A good coach is non-biased, non-judgmental, and 100% focused on *you*. The coach should have only one agenda: helping you achieve your goals.

It should go without saying that a good coach also understands the necessity of maintaining absolute confidentiality. And in most circumstances, the goal of a coach is to become "obsolete"—helping you to achieve what you want and establish new, positive habits and behaviors that you can sustain long-term—so that the coach is no longer required.

Interview a few coaches by phone or in person, and narrow down the field. Then, talk to their past coaching clients, if possible, and request a free trial session with the coach (sometimes called a "chemistry session"). A coach may have stellar credentials, but the chemistry between you needs to be spot-on in order for you to achieve your goals. You need someone who's right for *you*.

When you conduct your interviews, don't be afraid to ask tough questions. Here are a few you might ask an executive coach before you hire him or her:

- How long have you been an executive coach?
- What types of people and situations have you worked with?
- What kind of results did you achieve?
- Have you ever failed as a coach, and what were the circumstances?
- What is your coaching model and process?
- Where did you get your training?
- Is there anyone you would turn down as a client?
- What is your greatest strength as a coach?
- How would you describe your style as a coach?

You'll want to gather any and all facts that will inform your decision because you'll be making an important investment in your career. The cost varies widely across the world and depends on the coach's level of experience and track record. *Harvard Business Review* has reported that executive coaching rates range from about $300 to $3,500 USD per hour.

The questions I've listed will help ensure you get a good return on investment ("ROI"). Indeed, two large-scale independent studies of thousands of executive coaching clients worldwide found an ROI of 600-700% of the cost of their initial investment. That's an incredible testimonial for coaching, but just take care to choose your coach wisely.

If you do, you're almost certain to get more out of the experience than you expected.

You Don't Have to Go It Alone

Once you find an executive coach who will work well with you, the benefits can be enormous, whether you simply want to advance and grow in your profession or whether you have something specific you want to accomplish.

As Jack Canfield wrote in his book, *The Success Principles*, "Of all the things successful people do to accelerate their trip down the path to success, participating in some kind of coaching program is at the top of the list."

The bottom line is that a coach can be your greatest ally and can keep you from feeling as if you're out at sea in a boat by yourself. Remember: Executive coaching is not so much for leaders with problems as it is for people who want the most finely honed leadership skills possible. It's for leaders who truly embrace success.

Mastering Self-Leadership

As you work on fine-tuning the skills I've written about in this book, remember the importance of self-leading. Too often, it's overlooked as an aspect of total leadership, but in my experience of coaching hundreds of senior leaders, I have found that it's crucial to achieving increasingly greater roles and responsibilities in any organization ... and in your career as a whole.

Once you realize success isn't just about leading others but also about leading YOU™, the game changes. As you learn to manage your own behaviors and lead yourself as well as you lead others, your efficiency increases, your work relationships improve, your job satisfaction skyrockets, and your Executive Presence strengthens. And that's what builds your unique leadership brand both inside and outside of your organization.

Index

A

accountability buddy 136, 188–189
achievements 145–147
advocate engagement, as influencing tactic 172
apologizing 81–82
Apple 51, 89
arguments, benefits of 88–89
aspirations, career 156–162
authenticity 23–24
authority (subject), as influencing tactic 170

B

balancing acts
  intuition vs. analysis 149–153
  strategy vs. execution 56–57
  tasks vs. relationships 117, 123–124
  work vs. life 62–63, 78, 82–85
BCG (Boston Consulting Group) 101
behavior
  changing habits 185–187
  drivers 42–43, 87–88, 89–90
bias, unconscious 102–114, 168
biorhythms 72
black-and-white thinking 45–52
blame culture 92
Blanchard, Ken 175
blind spot bias 107
body language 80
bosses
  coaching "up" 120–122
  communication 117–119
  managing 85, 117–122
  saying "no" to 80
  visibility 143, 144–146

BP 196
brain, human 47, 107, 152
branding 16–19
Brock, Vikki 152–153
bullying 31

C

Canfield, Jack 199
career planning 156–162
CCODE 21–22
Center for Creative Leadership 164, 173
Chief Information Officers 130
Clance, Philine 130
coachability 14, 15, 23, 176
coaching, executive 193–194, 196–199
coaching "up" 120–122
collaborative influencing tactics 170, 172
commitment 21
  as influencing tactic 171, 174
communication
  small talk 124–127
  upward 117–119
competence 167
competition 171
complacency 177
Complete-Leader Model 153
compliance 173–174
confidence 32, 37–41, 130–133, *see also* Executive Presence
confidence journal 132–133
confirmation bias 110, 112
conflict 31–33, 58–60, 77, 86–98
conflict resolution 97–98
conquer response 35
consultation, as influencing tactic 172
cope response 34–35
courage 21, 51
cower response 34
creative thinking, *see* black-and-white thinking
criticisms 178, 180
culture, workplace 12, 92, 113
curse of knowledge bias 111, 112
CVs 146–147

D

decision-making 149–155
decisions, disagreeing with 34–36
defensive behavior 32
delegation 56, 73
delivery focus 53–55, 117
Details (Level of Focus) 95–96
discipline 22
diversity 99–101, 194–195, *see also* bias, unconscious
Dominican University of California 188
Drama (Level of Focus) 91–93, 168
Dyer, Wayne 51

E

ego 17, 176
email management 71–72, 85, 140–141
emotional influencing tactics 170, 171–172
empathy, as influencing tactic 171
employee loyalty 195
End-Point Exercise 158–161
energy 22, 47, 72, *see also* biorhythms
excuses 38
execution focus 53–55, 117
executive coaching 193–194, 196–199
Executive Leadership Brand, importance of 16–18
Executive Presence 128–136
expertise, as influencing tactic 170

F

factual data 98, 113, 140, 150–151, 168, 170, *see also* Details (Level of Focus)
fairness 167–168
fear-based behavior 27–36, 67–68
fear of failure 38, 51, *see also* Impostor Syndrome
feedback 132, 175–181, 186, 190–191
fist over fist visual illustration 32–33
Five Levels of Focus 91–97
flattery, as influencing tactic 171
flexibility 48, 50–51, 168
Focus, Five Levels of 91–97
Fogg Behavior Model 186
friendship, as influencing tactic 172
fundamental attribution error bias 111–112, 112

G

Gandhi, Mahatma 188
Gates, Bill 89
Getty, John Paul 61
globalization 99–101, 194
goal-setting 145–146, 157, 162, 182–189
Godin, Seth 39
gossip, *see* Drama (Level of Focus)
gray areas 46–47, 48–49, *see also* black-and-white thinking
gut instinct 121, 150–153, 155

H

halo effect bias 111, 112
harassment 31
Harvard Business Review 167, 198
Harvard Business School 166
health 22, 77
Hugo, Victor 51–52

I

Imes, Suzanne 130
Impostor Syndrome 130
Influence Toolbox 169–173
influencing skills 163–174
in-group/out-group bias 110–111, 112
inner voice 38, 39–41
interlocked hands visual illustration 33–34
interviews 147–148
intuition vs. analysis 149–153

J

Jefferson, Thomas 176
Jobs, Steve 89
Jordan, Michael 183–184

K

Kandola, Binna 103, 110

L

Lafley, AG 161–162, 192–193
leadership branding 16–17

leadership models 153
leadership skills, hard and soft 129–130, 194, 195
Levels of Focus 91–97
likability 167
limiting behaviors 15, 26
LinkedIn 148
listening 81, 126, 168, 178
logical influencing tactics 170–171
Long, John Luther 22
loyalty, employee 195

M

managing across 117, 120, 122–123
managing up 80, 85, 117–122
M-A-T Model 186–187
meeting management 67–71, 144–145
mentors 136, 181
Microsoft 89
mind management 37–44
modesty, *see* self-promotion
Motivational Balance Sheet 153–155
motivation (to change behavior) 186–187, 188
multi-tasking 71, 73–74

N

names, remembering 126–127
networking 122–127
"no", saying 70, 72, 76–85

O

objectives, *see* goal-setting
openness 21
organizational structures 118, 164, 194

P

Pearce, Robyn 75
peer management 117, 120, 122–123, *see also* networking
people-leadership behaviors 11
Pepper, John 12–14, 176
perceptions
  of others 17–18
  victim mentality 29–31

performance reviews 139–140, 140, 145–146
Peter, Laurence J. 157
Planning (Level of Focus) 94–95
praise 140, 171
Presence, Executive 128–136
pressure, as influencing tactic 171–172
pride 176
priorities 72, 73, 74
problems
  communication with bosses 117–118, 119, 145
  focus on 93
  responses to 34–36
  solving 47
  strategic thinking 57–58, 60
Problems (Level of Focus) 93, 168
Procter & Gamble (P&G) 12–13
Proctor, Bob 188

Q

questions
  feedback surveys 178, 179–180
  phrasing 81, 120, 125, 126, 168
  to ask executive coach 198
quit response 35

R

reciprocity, as influencing tactic 172
recruitment 109, 110, 147–148
relationships 122–124, 166–167, 172
reminders, goal 187
resistance 173
respect 168
resumes 146–147
right and wrong 107, 110, *see also* black-and-white thinking
risk-taking 47
Rock, David 91
role models 136
rules, rigid adherence to 45–46

S

Sale, Nic 103

self-assessments 21, 22, 146
  black-and-white thinking 49–50
  career planning 159–160
  Executive Presence 134–136
  influencing skills 165
  strategy vs. execution 56–57
  tasks vs. relationships 123–124
  time management 63–67
self-confidence 32, 37–41, 130–133, *see also* Executive Presence
self-leadership
  and branding 18
  common characteristics 24–25
  importance of 11–12, 199
  limiting behaviors 15–16, 26
self-promotion 118, 137–148
silo mentality 58–60, 91
similar-to-me bias 109, 112
small talk 124–127
social validation, as influencing tactic 171
stakeholders
  and increased visibility 143
  feedback from 177–178
  relationships 123–124, *see also* networking
Starbucks 18–19
strategic thinking 53–60, 94, 95

T

tasks vs. relationships 123–124
thinking vs. doing 56–57
thoughts, power of 43–44
three-brain model 152–153
time logs 63–67
time management 61–75
to-do lists 74, 78
Tolstoy, Leo 11
triggers 187
trust 168, 171, 190, 191–192
turnover, employee 195

U

upward management 80, 85, 117–122
us vs. them, *see* you vs. me mentality

V

vacations 82–85
victim mentality 27–36, 67
visibility 118, 142–146, 148, 191
Vision (Level of Focus) 94, 95
voice-activated software 72

W

Waitley, Denis 29
warmth 166–167
Western Leadership Model 153
"What You Think is What You Get" Triangle 42–43, 87–88, 89–90
work vs. life balance 62–63, 78, 82–85
Would YOU Want to Work For YOU™ 11, 73

Y

YOU™ 16, 20–21
you vs. me mentality 31–33, 57–58, 121

About the Author

International leadership and branding expert, Brenda Bence, is an Executive Coach who has worked with more than 700 senior leaders in dozens of the world's largest and most recognized companies. *Leadership Excellence's* annual Leadership 500 ranking has recognized Brenda's proprietary leadership development programs as one of the top 25 in the world for Independent Trainers/Coaches.

Given her MBA from Harvard Business School and her real world executive experience with companies like Procter & Gamble and Bristol-Myers Squibb—where she was responsible for billion-dollar brands across four continents and 50 countries—Brenda understands the challenges of today's global working environment.

For the past 15 years, Brenda has been running her own business—Brand Development Associates (BDA) International, Ltd.—from offices in both the U.S. and Asia. Besides her individual and leadership-team coaching services, she is an in-demand professional speaker and trainer at conferences, conventions, and company meetings across Southeast Asia, Greater China, the U.S./North America, Western & Eastern Europe, the Indian Subcontinent, Australia/New Zealand, South America, and Africa. She has presented her dynamic programs for such clients as Abbott, Bank of America Merrill Lynch, Boston Consulting Group, Citi, Credit Suisse, Danone, Deloitte, General Electric, KFC,

Kraft, Lilly, Mattel, Microsoft, Morgan Stanley, Pizza Hut, Royal Bank of Scotland, Radisson, Sheraton, Standard Chartered Bank, and UBS AG.

Brenda is the author of *Would YOU Want to Work for YOU™?*, *Master the Brand Called YOU™*, *Smarter Branding Without Breaking the Bank*, and the *How YOU™ Are Like Shampoo* series of personal branding books, which have collectively won over 30 national and international book awards. As both a magazine and a newspaper columnist, Brenda has written articles related to leadership, branding, and executive coaching that have been published in more than 400 media outlets such as *Investor's Business Daily, Affluent, The Financial Times, The Los Angeles Times, Entrepreneur, Kiplinger's Personal Finance, Reader's Digest, Cosmopolitan,* and *The Wall Street Journal's SmartMoney.*

A popular guest on television and radio, Brenda has sat on boards of both public and private companies, as well as not-for-profit organizations. She has travelled to 90 countries, is an avid Mahjong player, and enjoys studying foreign languages.

Visit www.BrendaBence.com to find out more.

Acknowledgments

My ideas usually come not at my desk writing, but in the midst of living.
—Anais Nin, American Author

Of all of the books I've written, both *Leading YOU™* and its companion book, *Would YOU Want to Work for YOU™?*, are the two for which this quote above holds most true. Years of work and thousands of hours of coaching have brought *Leading YOU™* into existence. I am extremely grateful to each and every executive I have had the privilege of coaching throughout the years. They openly shared their successes and trials, dreams and challenges. Without them, this book would not exist.

Many thanks also go to the following talented group of individuals who have lent their considerable skills to help this book morph from a series of ideas into reality:

- Melanie Votaw for her dedication and patience throughout the writing and editing process
- George Foster for his great cover design, never-ending flexibility, and consistent willingness to keep working at it "until it's just right"
- Eric Myhr for his outstanding typesetting services and unflappable positivity
- Swas "Kwan" Siripong for his excellent graphic design work and quick response time

- Graham Dixhorn for his book-cover writing skills and Mary Mihaly for her early-on editing work

Besides those who actually worked "on" the book, there were many people who supported me throughout the process of this book's development. In particular, my sincere gratitude goes to:

Daniel Jackman, my partner in life and business, whose presence and humor blesses me every single day—thank you!

Jagdish ("Jag") Gill, Associate at BDA International, for your strong support and "can-do" attitude—what a joy it is to have you on board!

My Team—I am eternally grateful.

Services Provided by Brenda Bence

Executive Coaching

Brenda has coached more than 700 senior leaders representing over 60 nationalities across six continents and 70 different industries. She offers in-person, video, and telephone coaching to C-Suite Executives, Senior Leaders, Business Owners, and Board Members located anywhere around the world. With 20 years of both internal and external coaching experience, Brenda provides perspective and encouragement—much like having a partner "running alongside you" at work—as you put your Executive Leadership Brand into action. Just as a personal trainer helps you craft a plan to reach pre-defined fitness goals and then stretches you to reach those goals, Brenda works with you to think *bigger* and helps you break down objectives into actionable steps that allow you to become the leader you want to be.

Brenda is a Certified Coach with the International Coach Federation and with Results™ Coaching Systems (Australia), and she is a member of the Asia Pacific Alliance of Coaches. She also serves as an Adjunct Coach with the Center for Creative Leadership. She sits on corporate coaching panels for multinational corporations based in London, Zurich, Singapore, New York City, and Hong Kong.

Professional Speaking Engagements

Brenda is in demand as a conference, convention, and corporate speaker, not only for her unique approach and powerful content related to leadership development and corporate and personal branding, but also for her warm, dynamic, and engaging style. Her popular one- or two-hour keynote addresses "enter-train" your group as she shares enlightening and humorous stories from her years as a corporate leader and Senior Executive Coach. Her practical, no-nonsense approach provides every participant in the room with strategies they can put into action the minute they walk out the door.

Brenda is one of only a fraction of speakers worldwide who have earned the two highest designations awarded in the professional speaking industry: the Certified Speaking Professional designation from the National Speakers Association and the CSPGlobal designation from the Global Speakers Federation.

Corporate Workshops

Brenda's interactive corporate programs will change the way you and your team look at leadership and branding. Customized for the specific needs of your organization, Brenda offers both half-day and full-day programs on a variety of self-leadership and leadership development topics including, but not limited to: Boost Your Executive Presence, Master the Brand Called YOU™, Would YOU Want to Work for YOU™? (Effectively Leading Others), Increasing Your Organizational Savvy, On-the-Job Coaching for Greater Success, Managing Tough Feedback, and Leading in Today's Multicultural / Multigenerational Workplace.

With Brenda's workshops, one thing is guaranteed: Participants don't just sit on the sidelines and watch. Each attendee is highly involved in the learning process and will apply their new skills to actual day-to-day challenges they encounter at work.

Visit www.BrendaBence.com or write Brenda@BrendaBence.com for more information.

www.ingramcontent.com/pod-product-compliance
Lightning Source LLC
Chambersburg PA
CBHW061300110426
42742CB00012BA/1998